MACMILLAN MODERN DRAMATISTS

THE 'NEW DRAMA' 1900–1914

Harley Granville Barker,
John Galsworthy,
St John Hankin,
John Masefield

Jan McDonald
Professor of Drama,
University of Glasgow

M

First published 1986

Published by Higher and Further Education Division
MACMILLAN PUBLISHERS LTD
Houndmills, Basingstoke, Hampshire RG21 2XS
and London
Companies and representatives
throughout the world

Typeset by Type Generation Ltd,
London EC1

Printed in Hong Kong

McDonald, Jan
The 'New Drama' 1900-1914. — (Macmillan modern dramatists)
1. Galsworthy, John, 1867-1933 — Criticism and interpretation.
2. Granville-Barker, Harley — Criticism and interpretation.
3. Hankin, St John — Criticism and interpretation.
I. Title
822'.912'09   PR6013.A5Z/

ISBN 0–333–30873–5
ISBN 0–333–30874 Pbk

Macmillan Modern Dramatists
Series Editors: *Bruce King* and *Adele King*

Published titles

Reed Anderson, *Federico Garcia Lorca*
Eugene Benson, *J. M. Synge*
Renate Benson, *German Expressionist Drama*
Normand Berlin, *Eugene O'Neill*
Michael Billington, *Alan Ayckbourn*
John Bull, *New British Political Dramatists*
Denis Calandra, *New German Dramatists*
Neil Carson, *Arthur Miller*
Maurice Charney, *Joe Orton*
Ruby Cohn, *New American Dramatists, 1960–1980*
Bernard F Dukore, *American Dramatists, 1918–1945*
Bernard F Dukore, *Harold Pinter*
Arthur Ganz, *George Bernard Shaw*
James Gibbs, *Wole Soyinka*
Frances Gray, *John Arden*
Julian Hilton, *Georg Büchner*
David L Hirst, *Edward Bond*
Helene Keyssar, *Feminist Theatre*
Bettina L Knapp, *French Theatre 1918–1939*
Charles Lyons, *Samuel Beckett*
Jan McDonald, *The 'New Drama', 1900–1914*
Susan Bassnett-McGuire, *Luigi Pirandello*
Margery Morgan, *August Strindberg*
Leonard C. Pronko, *Eugène Labiche and Georges Feydeau*
Jeanette L Savona, *Jean Genet*
Claude Schumacher, *Alfred Jarry and Guillaume Apollinaire*
Laurence Senelick, *Anton Chekhov*
Theodore Shank, *American Alternative Theatre*
James Simmons, *Sean O'Casey*
David Thomas, *Henrik Ibsen*
Dennis Walder, *Athol Fugard*
Thomas Whitaker, *Tom Stoppard*
Nick Worral, *Nikolai Gogol and Ivan Turgenev*
Katharine Worth, *Oscar Wilde*

Further titles in preparation

MACMILLAN MODERN DRAMATISTS

Contents

List of Plates

Acknowledgements

I should like to thank the staff of the Enthoven Collection of the Victoria and Albert Museum, of the British Library and of the British Theatre Association; William Gaskill, director of *The Madras House* for the National Theatre, and Deidre Clancy, the designer, for granting me interviews; the staff of the Royal Shakespeare Company for making available material relating to the production of *The Marrying of Ann Leete* and of the National Theatre for similar material relating to *Strife*; the BBC for allowing me to view several times the recordings of *The Voysey Inheritance* and *Waste*. I am grateful to the Court of the University of Glasgow for allowing me a term's study leave to complete the book, and to Fiona Selkirk of the Publications Office for providing me with a hide-out in which to do so. Thanks are also due to my colleagues who read and offered advice on the manuscript in various stages of its completion, the late Professor J.F. Arnott, Greg Giesekam, Dr R.J. Lyall and Claude Schumacher, and to Joyce Allen and Valerie Eden who typed it. Above all, I should like to convey my gratitude to Sarah Mahaffy for her encouragement, her constructive criticism and her never-ending patience.

To
Ian, Katie and Anne-Marie, in spite of whom . . .

Editors' Preface

The *Macmillan Modern Dramatists* is an international series of introductions to major and significant nineteenth and twentieth century dramatists, movements and new forms of drama in Europe, Great Britain, America and new nations such as Nigeria and Trinidad. Besides new studies of great and influential dramatists of the past, the series includes volumes on contemporary authors, recent trends in the theatre and on many dramatists, such as writers of farce, who have created theatre 'classics' while being neglected by literary criticism. The volumes in the series devoted to individual dramatists include a biography, a survey of the plays, and detailed analysis of the most significant plays, along with discussion, where relevant, of the political, social, historical and theatrical context. The authors of the volumes, who are involved with theatre as playwrights, directors, actors, teachers, and critics, are concerned with the plays as theatre and discuss such matters as performance, character interpretation and staging, along with themes and contexts.

BRUCE KING
ADELE KING

Introduction

The 'new drama' movement emerged in the British theatre in the 1890s, and flourished in the first decade of the twentieth century. Its principal exponents were the playwrights, Harley Granville Barker, John Galsworthy, St John Hankin and John Masefield. G.B. Shaw, a firm supporter and promoter of the works of these dramatists, was atypical of the 'new drama', his own plays being of such an individual style that they cannot truly be described as belonging to a particular school. Critics such as William Archer, J.T. Grein and A.B. Walkley helped to further the principles of the 'new dramatists' in their reviews, and in the case of Archer and Grein, took an active part in the staging of their work. The philosophy common to all those involved included first, a belief in the importance of the theatre as a social force rather than as a social event; secondly, a desire to experiment with new dramatic forms and to break away from the rigid structure of the conventional 'well-made' play that dominated the commercial stage; thirdly, to make the theatre a reflection of everyday life rather than a closed, unreal, 'limelit' world; and finally, to create a more intellectually demanding literary drama than was currently available on the West End stage.

What had begun as a 'new drama' movement soon became a new theatre movement, for it was clear that the 'new drama' could not develop in existing theatrical conditions. The increasing commercialism of the West End stage which led to the long-run system and the domination of autocratic actor-managers was hardly conducive to any kind of dramatic experimentation.

For the 'new drama' to succeed it had to create its own theatrical environment. A number of small societies was founded with the purpose of presenting to a British audience the best of Continental drama, for example, the plays of Ibsen, Maeterlinck, Hauptmann and Brieux, and of encouraging English playwrights to write serious literary pieces for the stage. The first of these was J.T. Grein's Independent Theatre Society (1891), modelled on Antoine's Théâtre Libre in Paris, followed by William Archer's New Century Society in 1898 and the Stage Society, in which Shaw and Granville Barker played a major part, in 1899. These paved the way for the Vedrenne-Barker management at the Court Theatre which, in 1904, became the first permanent home for the 'new drama', and was regarded as the first step towards the creation of a National Theatre, the ultimate goal of all the supporters of the 'new drama' movement, and of Barker and William Archer in particular.

The 'new drama' movement has ideological links with other political and intellectual preoccupations in the 'nineties, with, for example, the growth of the discipline of sociology, exemplified by the works of Sidney and Beatrice Webb (*History of Trade Unionism and the Industrial Revolution*, 1894–8) and of Charles Booth (*Life and Labour of London People*, 1892–1903). Many of its pioneers, including G.B. Shaw and Granville Barker, were closely involved in the Fabian Society, founded in 1884, which advocated gradual social reform to be effected by the permeation of local and national government by intelligent radicals, armed with irrefutable statistical evidence on every kind of social injustice. Like the supporters of the 'new drama' movement, the members of the Fabian Society were mostly middle-class intellectuals.

The 'eighties and 'nineties also saw the extension of the Trade Union movement, culminating in 1900 in the Labour Representation Committee, the precursor of the Labour Party, which won a substantial number of seats in Parliament at the General Election of 1906, when the Liberal landslide victory after years of Tory rule offered the hope of a coherent programme for social welfare. During the period from 1880 to the turn of the century three new universities were established; Manchester, Birmingham and the University College of Wales. An awakening of social consciousness coupled with a sense that society was about to cross the threshhold of a new century, was expressed in the appending the adjective 'new' to anything that seemed to promise reform of the old order that was passing. The 'new drama' is part of the ethos that created the 'new Unionism', the 'new Realism', the 'new periodicals', such as *The New Age* and *The New Review* and, of course, the 'new woman'. The movement towards the emancipation of women, pioneered by Mary Wollstonecroft and John Stuart Mill, gained impetus in the last two decades of the nineteenth century which saw the more widespread use of birth control among the upper and middle classes, the affirmation of the property rights of married women by the act of 1893, the growing number of women in paid employment, resulting from the inventions of the typewriter and the telephone and the growth of large department stores, and the participation of women in sports, such as bicycling (which brought them increased mobility), tennis and golf, which demanded a change in fashion away from the inhibiting highly-corseted Victorian gowns towards lighter, shorter, ready-made clothes. The desire for the vote as a symbol of social worth which had been expressed in and out of Parliament from 1870 became more vociferous. In 1897, the National Union of Women's Suffrage Societies was formed to unite all the small women's suffrage organisations. Six years later Mrs Pankhurst and her daughter, Christabel, formed the more militant Women's Social and Political Union. Like the Fabian Society, the WSPU was predominantly a middle-class organisation. The Suffragettes' campaign did not reach its full force until 1912–13, with criminal violence on one side and inhuman penal laws on the other, but the re-evaluation of the role of women in society was a 'burning issue' during the time when the 'new dramatists' were writing. It was in this climate, then, that the idea flourished that the theatre, if not a platform for reformist propaganda, had at least the duty to raise social and moral consciousness and to play a part in necessary social change.

A model for such a drama, it was believed, existed in the works of the Norwegian dramatist, Henrik Ibsen (1828–1906), perhaps the greatest single influence on the 'new drama' in England. His work had been made known in the 'eighties by translations by Edmund Gosse and William Archer, but his real impact on the British theatre came with the performance of *A Doll's House* in 1889, presented by the actress, Janet Achurch and her husband, Charles Charrington. This was followed by a private production of *Ghosts*, banned by the Lord Chamberlain in 1891, and by a production of *Hedda Gabler* by the American actress, Elizabeth Robins, in the same year. Although Ibsen denied throughout his life that he was primarily a social philosopher and was opposed to his plays being treated as

4

propagandist pamphlets rather than as dramatic art, British critics tended to stress in their reviews the sociological aspects of his work. The first translation of *A Doll's House* into English by Mrs Henrietta Frances Lord was prefaced by an essay on women's rights. Shaw's *The Quintessence of Ibsenism* (1891), originally delivered as a lecture to the Fabian Society as part of a series entitled 'Socialism and Literature', interpreted Ibsen's plays as severe indictments against the tyranny of social conventions that destroyed the identity of the individual. 'Ibsenism' came to mean three things; a belief in a socialist political philosophy; a resistance to unthinking adherence to social convention; and, closely allied with that, a belief in a new role for women in society. These doctrines and the effect of the productions of Ibsen's plays blew through the theatrical establishment in England like a brisk storm wind. It became clear that the theatre could be used as a forum for serious thought and was not merely a place for escapist entertainment. Distinguished men of letters as well as young aspiring authors turned to the drama as a means of expressing their ideas.

The 'new dramatists' present a criticism of contemporary society in their plays, although none was explicitly propagandist and, unlike Shaw, they did not seek to turn the stage into a political platform. Although Galsworthy's *Justice* could be regarded as the polemical piece *par excellence* in that it was an important contributory factor to the penal reform relating to solitary confinement, both Galsworthy and Hankin express the view that the dramatist's business was to present life on stage as he saw it, and to leave to the audience the task of drawing any moral conclusion implicit in the play. The sociological aspect of the drama arose, according to Galsworthy, from the fact that a faithfully drawn picture of contemporary society was represented.

Each of the dramatists presented his vision of that society in an individual way. Barker's recurrent metaphor for the decay of the old order is a House or Family, that has to be regenerated by the personal courage, social commitment and intellectual integrity of a young person, someone who, to use his own words, is not 'careful with his or her life'. Galsworthy seeks a change in the *status quo* not by revolutions or by political campaigns but by an increase in those in power of toleration, sympathy, understanding and imagination, qualities vitally necessary to the well-being of society. Hankin, in his comedies of manners, highlights the absurdity of conventional social attitudes, particularly to women and to marriage. Barker, too, in his four major plays, but most comprehensively in *The Madras House* confronts the 'woman question', and Galsworthy, although the plight of all classes of women in early twentieth-century society is not a central theme in his work, addresses the problem of the double standard of behaviour expected by society of its male and female members in *Justice* and in *Strife*.

The socially critical nature of much of the 'new drama', both continental and British, brought it into conflict with the censor, and plays such as Ibsen's *Ghosts*, Shaw's *Mrs Warren's Profession* and later, Granville Barker's *Waste*, were refused a licence for public performance and had to be presented privately to a 'club' audience. The 'new dramatists' battle with the Lord Chamberlain came to a head in 1909, with the setting up of the House of Commons' Select Committee on Dramatic Literature. Barker and Galsworthy were among the playwrights who gave evidence in favour of the abolition of the censorship on the grounds that since dramatists' works were subjected to the arbitrary taste of one man, who was an acknowledged figure of the establishment, frivolous plays that upheld the social *status quo* were passed, while a licence was denied to serious works of social criticism. The ambiguous outcome of the Select Committee's enquiry changed little, although the appointment of a panel of readers marginally improved the situation.

Ibsen's influence on the 'new drama' movement in Britain extended further than the rather restricted view of his plays as social documents. His technique of using naturalistic settings and properties as vehicles for symbolic meaning to convey thematic significance was adopted by Barker, by Hankin and by Galsworthy, who defined Naturalism as 'the art of manipulating a procession of the most delicate symbols'. In this respect the 'new dramatists' owe more to Ibsen's dramatic method than to that of the French Naturalist movement, although Antoine's Théâtre Libre, with Emile Zola as its literary inspiration, had been the model for Grein's Independent Theatre Society. While espousing the cause of a 'free theatre', Grein explicitly dissociated himself from the extremes of French Naturalism, '*rosserie*', as it was called, advocating 'realism, but realism of a healthy kind'.

Much of the work of Barker, Galsworthy and Hankin can be termed 'naturalistic', in that it seeks to avoid the false theatricality of the 'well-made' play with its mechanical four-act structure, composed of Exposition, Complication, Obligatory Scene and Dénouement, a rigidity of form which reflected in the content of the plays an unreal and repressive view of society and social problems. Hankin, for example, advocated an 'open-endedness' in his plays, deliberately avoiding the conventional 'happy ending' of the commercial theatre, that is, a marriage. Most stage marriages, as he demonstrated comically in his *Dramatic Sequels*, were in realistic terms doomed to disaster, and he believed, therefore, that he was presenting a more optimistic view of the world (indeed a 'happier' ending) by avoiding the conventional marital conclusion.

The 'new drama' in England was also naturalistic in the sense that the plays presented ordinary people, usually the professional middle classes and their employees, going about their everyday affairs. They are seen eating and drinking, working, reading, sewing and chatting. The dramatic action takes place mainly in the homes of such people or in their offices, all carefully presented and full of the paraphernalia of everyday living. The 'new dramatists' take great pains to present their characters in an appropriate *milieu* and to show them as natural products of their environment. We are told about the clothes they wear, the rooms they inhabit, the food they eat. Settings and characters are described in detail, Barker, in particular, providing his actors with a closely documented personal history on which to build their performance. The picture of the environment is filled in by frequent allusion to people and to events that are not shown on stage. The world of the play is not restricted to the stage action, but the events of the drama are seen in the context of a wider society.

While seeking to present a picture of a recognisable group of characters in their appropriate habitat, the 'new dramatists' retained a strict sense of dramatic form. Galsworthy, in particular, frequently used a tight symmetrical structure, notably in *The Silver Box* and in *Strife*, to highlight the differences and the similarities in his upper- and lower-class characters by the juxtaposition of contrasting scenes. Barker, in *The Madras House* and in the first three acts of *The Marrying of Ann Leete*, adheres rigidly to the classical Unity of Time. Further, the naturalistic detail in the work of all three dramatists is subordinated to, or used to underline, the expression of the play's ruling idea. There is always a pattern evident in the plethora of meticulously observed and recorded details.

All the plays abound in excellent parts for actors, for the dramatists eschewed the cardboard stereotypes that had led both to the type-casting and to the cult of 'personality' acting on the West End stage. They demanded truthful characterisation, the sense of being part of an ensemble and the intelligence to grasp the dramatist's attitude to what was being presented. In providing such plays the dramatists furnished the acting profession with works challenging to their talents, and, at the same time, the actors involved in playing in the 'new drama' encouraged the movement by their commitment and by their technical and creative skills.

Part 1
The Theatres

The Court Theatre (1904–1907)

Granville Barker's plan to mount a six to twelve months' season of 'the uncommercial drama', as he called it, at the Court Theatre was first mentioned in a letter to William Archer in April 1903. The season was to be operated on a short-run system, with a fresh play mounted every fortnight, concentrating on high quality plays and acting, and with no attempt at 'productions'. The aims were to encourage a vital national drama, in preparation for the long hoped for National Theatre, to create a class of intellectual play-goers and to offer more challenging opportunities to actors. A year later Barker was given the chance to put his ambitious plans to the test.

The lease of the Court Theatre had been bought by a business man, J.H. Leigh, to mount a series of Shakespearian productions starring his wife, Thyrza Norman. Archer advised Leigh to invite Granville Barker to direct the third of these, *The Two Gentlemen of Verona*, in April 1904. Barker agreed, on condition that he be allowed to present

11

six matinées of G.B. Shaw's *Candida* which had already been done by the Stage Society, bringing Barker much critical acclaim for his portrayal of the poet, Eugene Marchbanks. The success of the matinées encouraged Leigh and his business manager, J.E. Vedrenne, to agree that a season of plays directed by Barker should begin at the Court in the following autumn. George Bernard Shaw, who had become a close friend of Granville Barker after the *Candida* production, took an active part in the enterprise, providing excellent plays, sound advice and, from time to time, much needed financial assistance.

The two main predecessors of the Court venture were J.T. Grein's Independent Theatre Society, founded in 1891, and its successor, the Stage Society, which rose out of the ashes of Grein's enterprise in 1899. Barker himself was the first to acknowledge the debt which he owed to these pioneers. At the dinner held at the Criterion Restaurant at the close of the Court season in July 1907, he said, 'Our work is but the continuation of that begun by Mr Grein and the Independent Theatre, carried on by Mr Archer and the New Century Theatre and by that body which I am always to refer to as my father and mother, called the Stage Society.'[1]

The foundations laid by the societies was vital to the success of the Court experiment not only in creating a new audience sympathetic to the intellectual drama, but also in whetting the appetite of actors for more demanding work and in giving them experience of playing in a new and challenging repertoire. Some of the finest Court actors served their apprenticeship in the Stage Society or in one or other of the smaller societies that rose up in imitation of it. It was with the Stage Society that Barker learned the arts and skills of directing, for he worked not only on his own play, *The Marrying of Ann Leete*, but on pieces by

Maeterlinck (*Interior* and *The Death of Tintagiles*), by Brieux (*The Philanthropists*) and by Yeats (*Where there is nothing*).

The societies had had very serious problems of administration. They had no theatre of their own, no place to rehearse, insufficient financial resources to offer permanent contracts to actors and no regular director. The Court Theatre, in providing a permanent home for the 'new drama', seemed to many to have created 'the promised land of the London stage'.

The Court Theatre building, in Sloane Square, Chelsea, was a relatively small house, holding 642 seats. It was altered in the Spring of 1904 to make it suitable for J.H. Leigh's scheme to alternate the Shakespearian productions with amateur performances, and in the event, the alterations made it eminently suitable for Barker's kind of repertory system. The dressing rooms and the scene dock were enlarged, and a rehearsal room, with the exact proportions of the stage area, was added so that two plays could be worked on at the same time. The playing area was quite small, the proscenium arch being 21 feet wide, the stage 24 feet deep. A stock of scenery, properties and furniture was provided.

Despite Barker's original plan to have the maximum seat price fixed at five or six shillings, the prices at the Court were comparable with those in the West End theatre. It was expected that about £150-£160 would be taken at the box office at each evening performance. *Captain Brassbound's Conversion* was considered a financial failure at an average of £80 takings per performance. The expected box-office return for a matinée performance was £100.

The financial affairs of the Court Theatre were in the very capable hands of its business manager, J.E. Vedrenne. Barker paid tribute to his shrewd ingenuity and his business sense, his caution in financial matters and his meticulous accounting. Barker concurred in the need for economy, a view expressed in his postscript-prologue to his plan for a National Theatre, 'We regard economy not merely as a necessity likely to be forced on the Theatre for lack of lavish endowment, but as an indispensable means to an artistic end.'[2] It was against his principles as a director to spend vast sums on setting or on the employment of expensive star actors. Thanks to Vedrenne's financial genius, both he and Barker drew regular salaries and were able to demonstrate in 1907 that if the 'new drama' was not a goldmine, it was certainly a viable proposition.

The plays performed at the Court Theatre can be put into four categories. The first is the work of G.B. Shaw, whose plays demand separate treatment not only because they formed the bulk of the Theatre's repertoire – 701 out of 988 performances – but also because of their theatrical original-ity, their brilliant rhetoric and their challenging moral and social philosophy. Shaw overturned nineteenth-century dramatic form with the avowed purpose of reversing the social order implicit within it. The value of his work to the Court Theatre experiment was inestimable. The opportu-nities afforded to actors by the parts which he created and his talent as a director of his own work were additional contributions. The Court gave to Shaw the chance to have his work presented as he wished in a congenial environment without all the disagreeable features that he so despised in the commercial theatre, and on several occasions it was the brilliance of the Court actors that won the audience round to his iconoclastic tirades against social convention and accepted dramatic form.

Secondly, there were the plays by new young British authors, most notably Granville Barker, John Galsworthy, St John Hankin and John Masefield. Their plays presented in Desmond MacCarthy's words 'a critical and dissenting attitude towards contemporary codes of morality'.[3] Another play in this vein was *Votes for Women!* written by the actress, Elizabeth Robins, who in the 'nineties had taken a lead in bringing the plays of Ibsen to the London stage.

Thirdly, the new translations of Euripides' plays by Professor Gilbert Murray, a staunch friend of the management, provided a classical element in the repertoire. His lyrical renderings of the Greek texts gave actors opportunities for heightened non-naturalistic performances, for poetic delivery and for choral verse speaking.

Finally, the Court followed the ITS and the Stage Society in bringing to its audience the best of contemporary European drama. *The Wild Duck* was produced in 1905, and Mrs Patrick Campbell played the title role in *Hedda Gabler* in 1907. Plays by Hauptmann, Schnitzler and Maeterlinck, all favourite authors with the avant-garde societies, also found a place in the programme. The only obvious omission is Chekhov, which is surprising for his work was certainly known to the Stage Society, and there were translations available by Constance Garnett, the wife of Edward Garnett, a close friend and adviser to Galsworthy and to the 'new drama' movement. There is no doubt that Barker as a director whould have been very much in sympathy with the atmospheric naturalism of Chekhov's work, which in many ways resembles his own. The first production of a Chekhov play in Britain was *The Seagull* at the Glasgow Repertory Theatre, itself a 'child of the Court', in 1907. At the dinner marking the end of the three Court seasons, Edith Wynne Matthison paid tribute as an actress to the Court authors, 'Our authors have fitted us out with an entirely new gallery of theatrical types, freeing us from the conventional classifications which have done injustice for humanity too much on the English stage.'

The three principal features of the contemporary commercial theatre which the Court management challenged were the long-run system, the star system and the emphasis on lavish and expensive settings. All three were mutually dependent.

The long-run system had developed in the middle of the nineteenth century when managers, such as Charles Kean, had attempted by extending the number of performances to cover the expenses of elaborate and costly settings. Its effects on acting were deleterious to say the least. Prolonged repetition bred staleness and lack of spontaneity. One of the principal contributions of the Stage Society and others like it to the acting profession was that it gave actors, locked in the long-run system, a chance to develop their talents and extend their range of parts. In addition, there was little incentive within the long-run system to experiment with new or unusual plays. To mount a production as lavishly as fashionable West End audiences had come to expect was a major financial investment, and it was economic folly to take risks, especially in pre-subsidy days. The Court seasons were organised as a series of short runs of two or three weeks with revivals of plays that had proved particularly popular. A new play was usually introduced in a series of six or seven matinées, and if it proved successful it would be transferred to the evening bill, sometimes immediately, but more often at a later date, thus allowing the author time to re-write in the light of audience reaction. *Candida, John Bull's Other Island, You Never Can Tell, Man and Superman, The Voysey Inheritance* and *The Silver Box* were among those plays which were premièred at matinées and were later put into an evening bill.

The advantages to the actors were considerable. A regular change of parts brought interest and variety to the work, and the actor, like the author, had the chance to improve on his performance in the interval between productions. It was also challenging and taxing work, for frequently an actor's services were required both for the matinée and for the evening performance. In May 1905, for example, Nigel Playfair was Bohun in *You Never Can Tell* and Hodson in *John Bull* on the same day. Edith Wynne Matthison played Electra in the afternoons in January 1906, and then Mrs Baines in *Major Barbara* at night, but Granville Barker had the most arduous task, in May 1905, taking on John Tanner at the *Man and Superman* matinées and in the evenings playing Eugene Marchbanks in *Candida*. The artistic opportunities presented by such a programme, however, outweighed the pressures for the actors.

The religious avoidance of the long-run benefited the Court actors and authors immensely, but it meant financial loss, both to the management and to Shaw. There is little doubt but that *You Never Can Tell, Man and Superman* and *John Bull's Other Island* could have had respectable runs by West End standards, and it is another tribute to Barker and Vedrenne, and to Shaw, that the temptation to join the commercial ranks was resisted.

The Court also remained resolutely outside the star system. The presence of a star actor, who was very often also the actor-manager of the company, meant first, a restriction on the choice of repertoire, and secondly, that the production was organised in such a way as to highlight his performance at the expense of the rest of the company. One reason why plays such as Ibsen's *A Doll's House* and *Hedda Gabler* failed to find favour with the actor-managers was that none of them wanted to, nor indeed could afford to, allow his leading lady to appear in such dominant roles. The fact that the Court got rid of stars encouraged the spirit of cooperation and ensemble in the company, which was such a distinctive feature of its style, and it also gave freedom in the choice of plays which could be selected for production on their merits, not because they contained an obviously starring role for the actor-manager.

The Court management discovered that the stars did not pay. The audience became used to convincing and efficient ensemble playing by young actors and was not interested in watching a star go through his paces. As there were no stars, there were no star salaries. Edith Wynne Matthison referred to the 'economic equity' within the company in her tribute to the management at the celebratory dinner in 1907. Lillah McCarthy gave up the £30 per week which she was earning in Wilson Barrett's company to assume the Court 'Twelve-pound look', as she put it. Yet the stimulating work, the artistic challenge and the growing reputation of the theatre made actors eager to join the company. Even the rituals which accompanied 'star-gazing' in the West End were discarded. At the Court there was no playing of the National Anthem as a prelude to the evening's entertainment. It was not regular practice, except occasionally on First Nights, for the performers to take an Act Call, and in productions of the Greek plays there was not even an interval, just a three-minute break in the performance.

The Court Company appeared with 'stars' on only two occasions, when Ellen Terry took the part of Lady Cicely Waynflete in *Captain Brassbound's Conversion*, and when Mrs Patrick Campbell played Hedda Gabler. Ellen Terry's appearance was not a success because by this time she was having great difficulty in learning her lines, and even the Court ensemble cracked under the strain of the uncertainty. Mrs Patrick Campbell's Hedda was excellent, but apparently she did not stand out as being overwhelmingly more talented than the rest of the company.

In his letter to Archer, Barker had said that he was anxious to avoid 'productions'. By this he meant the elaborate and costly décor both for Shakespearian revivals and for society drama that prevailed on the West End stage in which the integrity of the text was sometimes sacrificed to visual splendour. It was the policy at the Court to concentrate on the play and on the acting, yet naturalistic plays demand considerable care in setting if the actors are to present life faithfully on the stage. This demand appears to have been adequately met. The production of *The Silver Box* was commended in the *Era* (29 September 1906) for 'careful setting and dressing', but as a rule, Court sets were not commented on by the critics, either favourably or otherwise. Robert Loraine, the distinguished American actor, who for a time played John Tanner in place of Barker, thought the scenery shabby, and Shaw too held this view. The settings for the Murray translations of Euripides, however, were commended. The set for *Electra* was likened to a Gordon Craig design, 'the half lights of a forest drawn to some extent according to the ideas of Mr Gordon Craig. The whole scheme is a happy compromise between modernity and a pedantic respect for antiquity' said the reviewer in *The Sketch* (24 January 1906). Care was taken, as in most of the naturalistic drama, to provide an adequate and appropriate setting for the play and the players, but on no occasion was scenery allowed to dominate. With the exception of Charles Ricketts who designed *Don Juan in Hell*, no designer or painter is credited in the Court programme. From the actors' point of view, the shift in emphasis was welcomed. Lillah McCarthy wrote, 'The stage was swept clear of costly properties and gorgeous scenery. In the old days, the acting was often thwarted by the scenic effects. In the new order we were taught that the play's the thing.'[4]

In addition to breaking the mould of the late nineteenth century theatre establishment by readjusting its priorities to give increased emphasis to the play text and its interpretation by a company of actors, the Court was the first permanent theatre to give the director a major role in the theatrical process. The rise of the director, beginning in effect with T.W. Robertson's work on his own plays at the Prince of Wales' in the 'sixties, was an obvious concomitant of the rise of the naturalistic theatre. The fitting of all parts to the whole, the creation of a stage environment, that reflected as far as possible a 'real' one, demanded the overall control of one man. Additionally, the rise of the 'new drama' with its difficult philosophical ideas and its complex literary style meant that a single interpreter was needed so that the performance achieved some kind of intellectual unity. The Stage Society and others had recognised the need for such a guiding spirit, but in the early days there were few who were qualified to take on the task. Yet as in so much of the Court's work the seeds were sown in the Societies that bore fruit in Sloane Square. It was common practice at the Stage Society to ask one of its members to direct a play, a practice which had given Granville Barker his first opportunity.

In his speech toasting the management at the Vedrenne-Barker dinner, Herbert Beerbohm Tree paid tribute to 'a presiding genius, a directing personality', Granville Barker, but he should have said two directing personalities, for Shaw's contribution to Court productions was by no means limited to providing it with excellent plays. He directed most of his own plays and received innumerable tributes from his actors. J.L. Shine, who played Larry Doyle in *John Bull's Other Island*, wrote, 'You are a man worth working for, and if your brilliant play is not efficiently rendered, we alleged actors and actresses deserve extermination, for your god-like patience and courteous consideration, combined with your skilful and workmanlike handling of detail has been a revelation to me.'[5] Annie Russell, in a talk entitled *GBS at Rehearsals of Major Barbara* in April 1908, said, 'I have never seen actors so cleverly handled. No-one taught, but we were always encouraged, always told "why". Our talents were never belittled and we were made to feel proud of our powers. This is one reason why the Court Theatre of London . . . has the reputation of "discovering" so many good actors.' The critics' recognition of Shaw's power as a director, is shown in the *Daily Chronicle*'s review of *Major Barbara* on 28 November 1905, 'That he does make people act as they never act elsewhere is at any rate one quite indisputable proof of Mr Shaw's genius'. For his part, he enjoyed the 'team spirit' of the Court company, and felt much more at home in Sloane Square than in the commercial theatres of the West End, where in his view his plays could never be given adequate presentation.

Shaw, apart from giving advice to others, kept his directing activities at the Court to his own plays. Responsibility for the direction of the Greek translations and the naturalistic drama fell to Granville Barker. Ironically, although Barker might justifiably be regarded as the first real 'director' of the twentieth-century British theatre, he would in no way have approved of the cult of 'Directors' Theatre' that has arisen since his time, for Barker's first principle was to bring to the audience through the performance an interpretation of the play that reflected in every possible detail the meaning of the playwright's text. He saw the task of the director as being 'to suggest, to criticise, to co-ordinate', and never to put his own personal stamp nor his own idiosyncratic interpretation on a production. This fundamental belief in the integrity of the playwright's text rendered him in some respects an ideal producer of the 'new drama'. The emergent dramatist knew that his work would be faithfully represented and would be neither marred nor indeed 'saved', by the tricks of a virtuoso director. Barker was anxious that his actors knew the text as well as he did, and he insisted that everyone concerned with the production was conversant with the full script and not only with his or her own part.

An excellent actor himself, Barker understood fully what the actor needed to know to work creatively, and it was from actors that he received his greatest praise. He regarded the fundamental requirement for the creation of a role as being the building up of biographical information, such as he provides in the stage directions in his own plays. Each character, to be true in the present, had to have a believable past and a credible life off-stage. He told May Whitty, who played Amelia Madras in *The Madras House*, 'From the moment you come in you must make the audience understand that you live in a small town in the provinces and visit a good deal with the local clergy: you make slippers for the church and go to dreary tea-parties.'[6] This build-up of the character's past and off-stage life shows that Barker was working along very much the same lines as Stanislavsky, whom he did not meet until 1914. There were to be no technical tricks, no superficial and conventional gestures, but every aspect of the actor's performance had to be based on his creation of the 'inner truth' of the character he was playing.

Not only the actor's individual gestures but the whole movement of the play was dictated by this 'inner truth' in Barker's productions. He seldom went to rehearsals with a full set of plotted moves that had to be rigidly adhered to by the actors. Rather he saw the 'blocking' as growing out of the evolving characterisation. The positioning on stage was very seldom imposed from without, but was dictated rather by the actors' inner necessity for movement and by the relationships built up between characters. The cast was never drilled into pretty stage pictures as was often the case in the productions of the martinet actor-managers. This is not to say that Barker did not demand discipline and concentrated work from his actors. Any suspicion of a lack of total commitment to the task in hand met with a very frosty response, but he saw the director as being a fellow worker in the company, not as a despot.

Understandably in a man who had been brought up in the hard school of William Poel – when Barker played Richard II for Poel's Elizabethan Stage Society he was made to sit in a room for three weeks learning the 'tunes' of his part – Barker was intensely concerned with the actors' diction. He did not look for the virtuoso rhetorical delivery which Shaw demanded, nor, as was to be made clear in his later Shakespearean productions, did he want 'the voice beautiful', but he did want the actor's voice to be such a well-trained instrument that it could convey by inflection an exact interpretation of thought. Just as he was quick to point out the importance of silences and pauses in individual speeches, he was also at pains to achieve an overall rhythm and phrasing in the production – another feature that he had in common with Stanislavsky who wrote at length about 'tempo-rhythm'. Barker's splendid sense of rhythm and stress is praised by Lewis Casson, an actor who, after his time at the Court, was closely involved with the provincial repertory movement in Glasgow and in Manchester. Achieving a rhythm suitable to a particular play depends very much on the actor's ability to feel the innate rhythm of his own part and to apprehend the rhythm of those he is playing with. However, some have criticised Barker's productions at the Court for being rather slow. *The Silver Box, Hedda Gabler* and *The Charity that began at Home* were all criticised for lack of briskness by several reviewers, and it is possible that in an attempt to 'think through' their lines and avoid the glibness of the West End, the actors overdid the pauses as they took time to think before they spoke and so obtain a truthful and spontaneous effect.

Barker's strength as a director lay in the naturalistic drama and his greatest triumphs at the Court were his own play *The Voysey Inheritance* and Elizabeth Robins' *Votes for Women!*. He was also most sympathetic to the style of Galsworthy and Hankin, and created for the audience, as Geoffrey Whitworth put it, 'a kind of spiritual realism, not only in the sphere of scenic representation, but even more important in that of acting'.[7]

Shaw had the highest admiration for Barker, but recognised that their directorial styles (and indeed their plays) were very different. 'Barker's production of his own plays and Galsworthy's were exquisite because their styles were perfectly sympathetic, whereas his style and taste were as different from mine as Debussy's from Verdi's.'[8] Occasionally Barker was too 'low-toned' for Shaw even in the direction of his own plays. 'Don't suppress your people too much', he warned Barker, after seeing *The Voysey Inheritance*, and he was never happy when he had to leave Barker to direct a Shavian play. Although Barker gave some excellent performances in Shavian parts – Eugene Marchbanks, Louis Dubedat and John Tanner – his 'implicit' style of direction could not deal satisfactorily with the gloriously 'explicit' nature of Shaw's plays overall. Their methods of working were also very different. Barker worked long hours, driving himself and his actors to the point of exhaustion. Shaw believed in rehearsing in the mornings only, leaving the actors time to digest his little notes for the rest of the day.

In the course of his career Barker came to the conclusion

that it was preferable not to be performing in the plays which he was also directing, and although he took several major parts at the Court, he did not appear at all in the Repertory Season at the Duke of York's, and virtually gave up acting in 1911 to concentrate on directing.

There is no doubt that the Court actors were extremely fortunate in having the combined, if differing, directorial talents of Shaw and Barker, and most of them were quick to appreciate the contrast between these two men and the West End actor-managers, rapping out commands from the stalls, treating the actors like pawns on a chessboard, telling them on which flower of the carpet to stand and, most important, failing to provide a congenial atmosphere for the flourishing of creative work.

The principal features of the 'house style' at the Court which the critics and the actors themselves described, were: first, a spirit of dedication and commitment to the ideology that inspired the 'new drama' movement; secondly, a high standard of ensemble playing; thirdly, a thorough and flexible command of the art of stage speech; and, finally, the ability to convince an audience of the inherent truthfulness of the characters and the life presented on stage.

A high proportion of the Court Company, both before and during their time with the Vedrenne-Barker management, appeared for the many stage societies which had sprung up in opposition to the prevailing commercialism of the contemporary stage. The importance of this experience is two-fold. In the first place, the Court actors were practised in playing in serious, non-commercial drama, and brought what they had learned to their Court performances. Secondly, they had given evidence of their commitment to improving the current state of the theatre. It was this reforming zeal that created the 'spirit' of the Court company that is so often referred to. Theodore Stier, the company's musical director, talks about 'a band of brothers who laboured so earnestly and with such intense enthusiasm',[9] and Edith Wynne Matthison, in her speech on behalf of the actors at the celebratory dinner which closed the season, describes 'the sense of human brotherhood and sympathy, firmly based on economic equity and artistic opportunity'.

The actors were, in addition, very much in sympathy with the radical social views expressed by the 'new dramatists'. One practical instance of this was the involvement of some of the leading members of the Court company in the reform of the Actors' Association, the forerunner of Equity, the Actors' Union, in 1907. The aim of the 'Reform Party', which included Barker, Henry Ainley, Edith Wynne Matthison and Clare Greet from the Court, was to prevent the Association from turning into a social club and to force it to consider seriously the financial difficulties of many members of the profession. Largely thanks to their initiative, the minimum weekly wage for a speaking part in London was established at £2 per week. Many of the actresses, including Lillah McCarthy and the actress-turned-playwright, Elizabeth Robins, were involved with the Actresses' Franchise League, the theatrical branch of the Women's Suffrage Movement. The will to reform the theatre went hand-in-hand with the will to reform the lot of the actor in society, and, indeed, society as a whole.

A common ideological base and a corporate sense of commitment to pioneering a new theatrical venture assisted in the attaining of the highest standard in ensemble playing so far achieved in the British theatre. Barker, in thanking his actors for their work over three Court seasons at the dinner in 1907 said, 'I would rather think of them as a company than as individuals, brilliant individually as they may be, for I feel very strongly that it is the playing together of a good company which makes good performances.' The whole organisation of the Court experiment was conducive to such an achievement. The 'new drama' provided more than one or two interesting parts, designed for the actor-manager and his wife; the absence of 'stars' meant a more balanced company; the short-run system meant that actors had the opportunity to play a variety of parts and were willing, as in the instance of the Police Court scene in *The Silver Box* to play 'extras' in one production although they had leading roles in another. The two directors, Shaw and Barker, both worked consistently to create an overall picture. Shaw's rehearsal notebooks abound in instructions to one actor to 'play to' another, and he was quick to berate in one of his 'little notes' any performer who was failing to react to his fellows. Barker's sensitive grasp of the overall rhythm of the play and his desire to present on stage everyday life in all its complex detail equally guided the company in the art of playing together and not as isolated individuals.

Another outstanding feature of the Court style was the clarity and beauty of the actors' diction. Barker, as Sydney Fairbrother reports, was himself 'crazy mad about elocution',[10] and according to two other distinguished Court performers, Lewis Casson and Louis Calvert, it was fundamentally in an ability to speak well that the success of the Court actors lay. 'Barker and Shaw would not have been able to achieve what they did had they not had at their disposal actors of a distinct type, trained speakers brought up in a tradition where there was an art of stage speech',[11] wrote Casson. One major contributor to this tradition was William Poel, whose emphasis on the 'tunes' of a play had a considerable influence on Barker, Lillah McCarthy and the others who worked with him. Speaking well, certainly in the context of the Court style, meant that through training one appeared to speak naturalistically. 'We may say', wrote Calvert, 'that our purpose is not to speak naturally on stage, but to make people think we are speaking naturally, and that comes as the result of study and hard work. The natural speaking voice is of little or no use on the stage.'[12] The plays in which the Court actors' diction was most commended were the Murray translations of Euripides, very lyrical and rhythmical renderings of the Greek texts. *Hippolytus* was called 'a festival of dramatic diction' (*The Sunday Times*, 23 October 1904) and praised for 'its finished yet unmannered declamation' (*Illustrated London News*, 29 October 1904). *The Trojan Women* was 'always rhetorically effective' (*Saturday Review*, 22 April 1905) and *Electra* was spoken in 'faultless yet full-blooded declamation' (*Illustrated London News*, 17 March 1906). Murray was delighted that 'Barker's production broke away from stilted formal speech, which, following the French tradition had dominated "classic" productions of the period'.[13]

The greatest challenge to the actors' powers of delivery came from the plays of G.B. Shaw. There were three difficulties to contend with: first, the length of the speeches, from the point of view of memory as well as of delivery; secondly, they contained difficult and often highly abstract arguments; and, thirdly, Shaw was writing in an Irish idiom which his English interpreters found it hard to cope with. 'One of the troubles is that his Irish melodies are often too long and elaborate for an English actor to retain or reproduce, and without them much of the significance and emotional appeal of the lines is lost',[14] wrote Lewis Casson. Shaw in his letters and his rehearsal notebooks expresses a wish for a 'bigger', a more rhetorical style of delivery than the actors were used to employing in modern plays. Barker did not escape Shaw's criticism in this regard. Shaw preferred actors with Lillah McCarthy's training in melodrama. 'Saturated with declamatory poetry and rhetoric from her cradle, [she had] learned her business out of London by doing work in which one was either heroic or nothing.'[15] Yet, although Shaw had reservations about his actors' delivery, the critics were quick to appreciate the eloquence and rhetoric of Louis Calvert and Ben Webster in *John Bull's Other Island* (1904), and Robert Loraine and Norman McKinnel in *Don Juan in Hell* (1907).

Part of the inspiration of the Free Stage Movement in Europe, Antoine at the Théâtre Libre, Otto Brahm's Freie Buhne and Stanislavsky's Moscow Art Theatre, had been a will to reform contemporary acting style. The continental acting manifestos were based on a theory of Naturalism, and the new style was most successfully employed in plays that demanded naturalistic acting. The similar movement in Britain had a more literary bias, partly because its instigators and pioneers were themselves men of letters or critics rather than theatrical practitioners like Antoine and Stanislavsky, but also partly because there was less of a need for reform in acting style as a result of the moves in that direction taken by the Bancrofts at the Prince of Wales' Theatre in the 1860s and '70s.[16] None of the many avant-garde Societies saw it as their primary aim to effect major reforms in acting, but saw their duty rather as being to provide for a growing body of talented and intelligent actors plays worthy of their gifts. In the naturalistic dramas of Galsworthy, Barker and Hankin, the Court actors were praised for their close observation of life and for their ability to portray what was observed in stage terms. Such meticulous observation was found in Edmund Gwenn's Relieving Officer in *The Silver Box*, which 'might have been – and probably was – studied from life', (*The Era*, September 1906), and his performance of Walker, the heckler, in *Votes for Women!*, when Max Beerbohm in the

Saturday Review (13 April 1907) complimented him on 'minute fidelity to the model, rolling gait, hands stuck down in his pockets, chin forward'. But the Court actor was not only faced with the problems of the naturalistic drama with its demands for inner psychological truth. There were the poetic and Greek dramas, and above all, there were the plays of Shaw, which formed such an important part of the repertoire. The naturalistic mode was not entirely appropriate for either genre. Shaw made that clear when he was directing his own plays. The actors, however, seem to have had the flexibility to adapt their naturalistic acting style and to overlay the 'inner truth' with what almost amounts to Brechtian 'alienation' or 'distancing' in Shaw's work, and with sensitive stylisation in the Greek plays. As far as playing in Shaw was concerned, it seems that the firm grasp of the 'inner truth' of the character helped the actors to avoid caricature. In 'showing' rather than 'being', it is too often the case that the type shown bears so little relationship to life, that it loses completely the social implications intended in the character. The Court Company used their powers of observation and their grasp of the 'inner truth' to create the role, and then broadened the interpretation sufficiently to convert it to a representation of a Shavian social type.

In *Candida*, Norman McKinnel is praised for 'having all the manners of the average clergyman, and none of the mannerisms of the stage parson' (*The Era*, November 1904). The doctors in *The Doctor's Dilemma* are described by Grein in *The Sunday Times* (25 November 1905) as being 'all specific and typical' – an excellent summing up of the aim of a Brechtian actor – and Desmond MacCarthy develops this point in his description of Eric Lewis's performance of Sir Ralph Bloomfield Bonnington as 'at once individual and typical, not a caricature'.[17] Occasionally critics fail to understand the extra layer that the actors had to assume to play Shaw correctly, and complain of the loss of naturalism. A review of *John Bull's Other Island* reveals such a misunderstanding, 'Messrs Granville Barker, A.E. George and Graham Brown are able to make fairly telling figures of domestic comedy until the author's freak forces them out of the natural groove.'[18] 'Out of their natural groove' is of course exactly where they should be, according to Brechtian theory. The achievement of a totally naturalistic effect was never Shaw's aim, and he was fortunate in being able to work with actors who realised that the naturalistic style in which they were so accomplished was only the necessary preliminary to the creation of a new style for Shavian drama.

The Court Company's dedication to the truthful application of observation to their parts also contributed to their playing in the Greek translations. 'Inner truth' was preserved, but style was not lost. On the basis of such 'truth', they were able to build up a poetic style, which kept the particular and psychological elements in the Greek plays, yet still allowed them to bring out the plays' more universal application. 'No-one sacrificed sound and rhythm to naturalness', wrote Max Beerbohm of *The Trojan Women* in April 1905.

Two comments by two faithful Court actors are relevant here, one by Lillah McCarthy, stressing the 'naturalness' of the Court acting, and one by Lewis Casson, stressing the style: first Lillah McCarthy, 'Whilst other producers were aiming at effect, truth was the effect at which the Court Theatre aimed.'[19] Lewis Casson explains the style in his comments on Desmond MacCarthy's tribute to the naturalness of the Court acting. This was 'an even better tribute than he imagined, for in saying that the acting was entirely natural, and not calculated for effect, he testified that what

31

was perhaps the most calculated and even stylised acting I have ever known succeeded in its effect'.[20] One of the major achievements of the Court actors was to develop the naturalistic style, initiated forty years earlier at the Prince of Wales', into a style of such flexibility that it could be employed not only in the naturalistic drama, but also, with modifications, to plays as widely different as those of Shaw and Euripides.

The activities of the Court actors, both during and after the Court seasons, show them to be a group of actors dedicated to the 'new drama', to the non-commercial theatre, to working with serious-minded directors rather than with autocratic actor-managers, preferably in a repertory or short-run system with emphasis on the text of the play and on acting rather than on expensive settings. They carried their theatrical ideals and their responsible social attitudes to the whole country and laid the foundations for the high standard of acting on which the reputation of the British theatre rested in the first half of the twentieth century.

The pioneers of the Independent Stage Society, the Stage Society and other similar groups not only provided the Court with playwrights, actors and directors, but also, initially at least, with its very special audience. The people who frequented the Court were 'very much of the kind which supported the opening experiments in the production of Ibsen', according to the *Athenaeum* (4 March 1905). That meant an audience of the Fabian, left-wing and largely middle-class intelligentsia, who were there to see a serious play finely acted, and not just to be seen at a glittering social occasion. While other theatre managers bewailed the fact that a persistent stream of late-comers disturbed not just the short piece inserted at the beginning of the programme to deal with just such a contingency but also the first act of the main play, Vedrenne had nothing to complain of in this respect. Plays at the Court were no sops to fashionable would-be 'cultured' London society, but were at one and the same time assaults on that very society and its anodyne drama. It is true that as the management became increasingly successful, the audience became increasingly fashionable. The Prince and Princess of Wales attended a performance of *John Bull's Other Island* in February 1905; the Bishop of London and A.J. Balfour were present at *You Never Can Tell* in 1906, and there was what was described as a 'brilliant audience, including the Prime Minister', at *Major Barbara* in November 1905, according to *The Times*. Shaw was not at all displeased by his growing 'fashionableness', for he was happy that the financial success of his plays should enable the management to subsidise matinées of plays by lesser known dramatists. The presence of the fashionable few never killed the intellectual expectations of the majority, and certainly did not make the management swerve from its avowed policy. The numbers grew because of the high standard of the product, not because of a weakening of the resolve to further the cause of the 'new drama' and to attack the unthinking adherence to accepted moral and social codes that, in the view of the Court dramatists and actors, brought misery and hardship in its wake.

The Court, despite its 'reforming' image, was never a 'popular', in the sense of a 'working-class', theatre. The plays all deal with the social and moral problems that confronted the middle classes at the time and, by the very statement of these problems, they sought to impress on the middle-class audience that the remedy for such social evils lay in their hands. Barker, Galsworthy and Hankin usually set their plays in the world of the affluent middle classes. They criticise this world for its hypocrisy, its lack of imagination, the inequity of its institutions which it too easily condones, and they, usually implicitly, demand reform, or at the least a reassessment of its values. Neither in content nor in form was the Court drama 'populist'. Its challenge was a challenge to the intellectual middle-class audience to recognise its social responsibilities.

The Savoy Theatre (1907–1908)

After the spectacular achievements of the Vedrenne-Barker management at the Court, the short season at the Savoy proved to be an anti-climax. Past success seemed to indicate that a move to a larger, newer theatre in the West End was the next step in the progress towards the establishment of a National Theatre. But the faithful audience of the Court had not grown enough to fill a theatre almost twice the size (the Savoy held 1,152), and the situation of the Court in Sloane Square, outside the West End orbit, had been one of its positive advantages as a home for the 'new drama'. There had always been an 'alternative' atmosphere at the Court, and when the management opened in the West End in a large modern theatre, and to boot, played the National Anthem at its first performance – 'a hideous solecism, a symptom of moral decay'[1], according to Shaw – it was not surprising that regular Court patrons found themselves at something of a loss.

The storming of the heart of commercial theatre-land was, however, regarded, initially at least, with some enthusiasm. Thanks to Shaw's generosity, the Savoy theatre was leased for less than £100 a week (a modest rent by West End standards) from Mrs D'Oyly Carte, and the opening of the Vedrenne-Barker season was announced for 16 September 1907. The Court formula of short evening runs and experimental matinées was continued. The company was drawn from the same group of actors who had gained such distinction at the Court: the programme of plays was chosen on the same principles. Productions of works by Shaw, Barker, Galsworthy and Masefield, a new translation of Euripides' *Medea* by Gilbert Murray, and Ibsen's *Peer Gynt* were planned. Yet the transplant failed, and not only because of the move to the West End.

The partnership between Barker and Vedrenne began to show cracks. The two men had never been close friends, but relations had always been amicable. Now for some reason, inexplicable even to Shaw, Vedrenne refused to cast Barker's wife, Lillah McCarthy, unless a playwright specifically asked for her services. Vedrenne may have been showing himself scrupulous in seeking to avoid the charge of nepotism, but Lillah McCarthy was, in her own right, one of the finest interpreters of the 'new drama' and had proved herself most particularly in her playing of Shaw's heroines. Vedrenne's intransigence meant that Masefield's new play *The Tragedy of Nan*, the dramatist's finest work, much praised by Shaw and Barker, was not performed at the Savoy. He was equally adamant that she should not play Medea in the Gilbert Murray translation, although she was very anxious to do so. Shaw, using his author's prerogative, managed to get her into the cast of the revival of *Arms and the Man* but could only win Vedrenne round by persuading Lillah McCarthy to take a very low salary – £25 for an engagement of twelve weeks. Such treatment was very distressing to an actress who had been one of the most distinguished and most loyal in the Court company, and it did not improve relations between Barker and Vedrenne. Additionally, Vedrenne was becoming increasingly engaged in other business interests. His new Shaftesbury Avenue theatre, ultimately called the

Queen's, was nearing completion and was absorbing more of his attention. As far as Barker was concerned the banning by the Lord Chamberlain of his play *Waste*, scheduled for production in the Savoy season, took from him all heart for the enterprise.

Shaw had a financial investment in the Savoy scheme, and his letters show him continually trying to whip up enthusiasm in the flagging managers, although he was less directly involved than he had been at the Court, believing that the 'new dramatists' could successfully mount their own plays without the aid of Shavian potboilers. The success of Shaw's plays, however, had made the Court Theatre financially viable as well as bringing to it artistic distinction. Further, Shaw, contrary to his practice at the Court, did not direct the three revivals of his plays that were staged at the Savoy, *You Never Can Tell*, *Arms and the Man* and *The Devil's Disciple*. He left this task to Barker, who, in Shaw's own opinion, was not a good director of Shavian drama. The Forbes Robertson production of *Caesar and Cleopatra*, 'imported' to the Savoy for a five week season was disastrous. Shaw had written the play for Forbes Robertson and Mrs Patrick Campbell as early as 1898, but it had lain untouched until Robertson wanted to tour it in America in 1906. Shaw had attended some rehearsals prior to the tour, but by the time it reached the Savoy the production was well below standard. In addition, it broke the continuity of the Savoy season, the house production, *The Devil's Disciple*, being transferred to Vedrenne's new theatre, The Queen's. This caused yet another rift between Vedrenne and Barker, as the latter had opposed the invitation to Forbes Robertson. *Caesar and Cleopatra* was also a failure financially, one that the management could ill afford.

A series of accidents, bad luck, bad management and bad

feeling put paid to the Savoy venture. There was no new Shaw play and the productions of the revivals lacked the distinction of the Court productions. The other 'new dramatists' fared badly, with Vedrenne's refusal of *The Tragedy of Nan*, the banning of Barker's *Waste* and the scathing reception given to Galsworthy's *Joy. Medea* was weakly cast, Edyth Olive giving a competent performance, but lacking in the 'barbarian savagery' that Lillah McCarthy would have brought to the part. Neither *Peer Gynt*, nor the Christmas pantomime, for which Shaw had pressed, was presented. The season ended on 14 March 1908 with the management bankrupt. Shaw personally bore the brunt of the financial loss.

The Vedrenne–Barker partnership was revived briefly in asociation with Frederick Harrison, manager of the Haymarket Theatre, in the summer of 1908. Barker was very reluctant but Shaw persuaded him to participate. *The Tragedy of Nan*, (Vedrenne having finally been brought round by Shaw), *Getting Married*, directed by Shaw himself, and eight matinées of *The Chinese Lantern* by Housman and Moorat made up the short season, which unfortunately proved to be another financial failure, particularly for Shaw. He was more disappointed, however, in the breaking up of the partnership which he had seen as the only hope for the promotion of the works of the 'new dramatists', for the establishment of a Repertory Theatre and for the ultimate goal, the National Theatre.

Frohman's Repertory Season (1910)

The next initiative to establish a Repertory Theatre in London came from an unexpected quarter. Charles Frohman, the American impresario, was persuaded by his friend, J.M. Barrie, to mount a season of plays in repertoire at the Duke of York's Theatre, of which he had held the lease since 1897. A fresh impetus was needed. Barker certainly felt that the 'new drama' movement was suffering for the lack of a home. 'All our lot of dramatists are slacking off in production because they can't be sure of anything but matinée audiences', he wrote to Gilbert Murray, 'Repertory is our salvation.'[1] The support of Galsworthy and of Shaw was quickly forthcoming. Shaw worked hard to involve Sir Arthur Wing Pinero, and even (in the end unsuccessfully) the latest theatrical *enfant terrible*, Edward Gordon Craig. The project was announced officially in April 1909. The stress on the new, and possibly unconventional, dramatist was emphasised in the Prospectus, 'A repertory theatre should be the first home of the ambitious young dramatist. I advise him to learn the conventions of the stage, but chiefly that he may be able to disregard them. One sometimes hears it said, "A good thing, but not a play". That is one of the kinds I want.'[2] Frohman did not think for one moment that good scripts alone made good theatre. He saw his repertory venture as involving the art of the actor as much as that of the dramatist, 'It will represent the combined resources of actor and playwright working with each other, a combination that seems to me to represent the most necessary foundation of any theatrical success.'[3] He was to be proved correct. The standard of acting at the Duke of York's constituted one of the project's most notable achievements.

The Prospectus announced a very ambitious programme, including new plays by Barrie, Barker, Gilbert Murray, Galsworthy, Laurence Housman, Henry James, John Masefield, George Meredith, Somerset Maugham, Arthur Pinero, Haddon Chambers and Shaw. There were to be revivals of Barrie's *Quality Street* and *What Every Woman Knows*, of Galsworthy's *The Silver Box* and *Strife*, of

Barker's *The Voysey Inheritance* and *Prunella* and of Shaw's *Major Barbara, Man and Superman* and *The Doctor's Dilemma*. Granville Barker and Dion Boucicault were to direct the plays, and Norman Wilkinson, who later made a major contribution to the success of Barker's Shakespeare productions at the Savoy, headed the team of designers and painters. A distinguished company of actors was assembled, including many veterans of Barker's seasons at the Court and the Savoy. The Duke of York's would be run as a true repertory theatre, not as a short-run theatre with experimental matinées as the Court had been.

The Repertory season opened on 21 February 1910 with the first production of Galsworthy's *Justice*, followed two days later by the first production of *Misalliance* by Shaw. On 1 March, the Triple Bill of *Old Friends* and *The Twelve Pound Look* by J.M. Barrie, and George Meredith's unfinished piece, *The Sentimentalists*, was introduced to the programme. Barker's *The Madras House* opened on 9 March and Pinero's *Trelawney of the 'Wells* on 5 April. The Triple Bill was then dropped, only *The Twelve Pound Look* being retained to accompany Barker's revival of *Prunella* on 13 April. *Helena's Path* by Anthony Hope and Cosmo Gordon Lennox opened on 3 May for only two performances. The death of Edward VII on 7 May closed the Theatre for a short period, but it opened again with *Trelawney* and *Prunella* playing in repertoire, together with Elizabeth Baker's *Chains*, introduced on 17 May. The season ended a month later. Frohman had by then lost a great deal of money. Indeed, had he been motivated solely by financial considerations he would have terminated the experiment much earlier, but partly his friendship with Barrie, and partly his desire for the artistic prestige that the repertory project brought with it, persuaded him to hold on, until the theatrical slump caused by the death of the monarch provided an acceptable pretext for closure.

Artistically the Repertory Theatre undoubtedly had its successes. *Justice* and *The Madras House* are two of the finest products of the 'new drama' movement. *The Twelve Pound Look* is an excellent one-act play. *Misalliance* is not one of Shaw's best works, but it is an interesting dramatic experiment, especially since at the Repertory Theatre it could be seen in tandem with *The Madras House* to which it is reputed to be Shaw's response. The only two *artistic* mistakes were *The Sentimentalists* and *Helena's Path*, but the only *financial* success was *Trelawney of the 'Wells* which had a total of 42 performances. (*Justice* had 26, *The Twelve Pound Look* 25, *Prunella* 17, *Misalliance* 11 and *The Madras House* 10). This was not even a new play, let alone an example of the 'new drama', and its author, Pinero, retained very serious doubts about the whole repertory project. He had refused to contribute a new play to the Duke of York's venture and had only reluctantly allowed *Trelawney* to be revived, having no wish, as he wrote to Shaw to 'cling desperately to the coat tails of the intellectuals'.[4] Established authors like Pinero and Haddon Chambers, whose name had appeared on the original list of authors, did not need, nor did they really want to be involved. They were at odds with the basic philosophy of the Repertory movement expressed by Barker in his essay on the subject in *The New Quarterly* (November 1909). 'A repertory theatre is a place frequented by people who take an interest in its work as its work, not visited occasionally for the sight of a popular success.' Pinero and others like him saw each play as standing or falling on its own merits, not as a part of a whole season, yet *Trelawney* owed its success in no small measure to the high standard of ensemble playing at the Duke of York's. 'Sir Arthur Pinero is not amongst the "literary" dramatists, and it was wonderful to see how his inelastic, sometimes stilted dialogue was pulled together and improved by the naturalistic acting of the Repertory Company.'[5]

Despite critical reservations about the inaccessibility or the gloominess of the plays, the brilliance of the acting was universally acknowledged. The nucleus of the company was composed of former Court Theatre players, and Mary Jerrold, formerly of Glasgow Repertory Theatre, and the young Sybil Thorndike were engaged for the season. The Court with its short-run system and experimental matinées had encouraged suppleness in the performer, and this experience provided an excellent grounding for actors participating in a repertory season. The variety of parts – some actors took as many as five or six different roles in the seventeen week season – was stimulating, but it was also challenging. In some instances major parts of great complexity were prepared for only ten or eleven performances. Acting in the Repertory Company required stamina, a complete mastery of varying styles and commitment. The actors transferred to the Duke of York's that spirit of dedication to the 'new drama' that had prevailed at the Court. The fact that the actors were working together as a permanent company for a season of plays, as they had never really been able to do at the Court, strengthened the ensemble playing, already recognised as a feature of the Court style. Further, they were accustomed to the directorial styles of Shaw, and of Barker, who was developing even further his technique of psychological realism in character creation, without losing his insistence on perfect diction. Dion Boucicault, whose experience had been in the commercial theatre, directed only the two Barrie one-acters and *Chains*, which proved a mistake, for Boucicault failed to achieve in his production the realism in either setting or playing demanded by the text. He was a martinet, insisting on perfect movement and perfect timing. coming to rehearsal with every detail worked out – a complete contrast to Barker. The incompatibility in directorial styles does not really seem to have caused great problems, and Barker could have had no complaints about Boucicault's performance as the Judge in his production of *Justice*, distinguished for its perfect diction.

Despite, however, the almost unanimous praise for the performance standard at the Repertory Theatre, William Archer[6] attributes part of the financial failure to the composition of the company. The actors, who had begun their careers at the Court as young, unknown and cheap, were now by reason of their training and of the reputation that the Court acting style had built, well-known and highly praised performers and therefore too expensive for the repertory movement. The Duke of York's, in Archer's view, ought to have relied on new promising young actors with commitment and should have sought to develop their talent, as the Court had done, rather than pay large salaries to established players. Archer also felt that the employment of 'stars' such as Dion Boucicault, Irene Vanbrugh and Lena Ashwell, was at cross-purposes with the repertory ideal. Stars were expensive and, in the Repertory Theatre, would not cover their salaries by attracting a huge personal following as they would in the commercial theatre. In addition, in the repertory system, actors had to be paid even when they were not playing, and this constituted yet another financial drain. The short life of the Repertory Theatre at the Duke of York's obviously depressed those who had participated in the hope that this venture would be a milestone on the road to a National Theatre. It certainly proved that a National Theatre demanded a large subsidy. Frohman hinted that he might mount a similar experiment in the following spring, but it did not materialise. Even his coffers were not bottomless.

Although the failure of the venture can be seen as attributable to financial reasons, there were also, as William Archer pointed out in his essay in the *Fortnightly Review*, defects in managerial policy and its implementation. He refuses to accept the most commonly held excuse, that the Repertory system just could not work in London, a view held by Barker, who was now convinced that the future of the repertory movement lay in the provincial cities. He agreed, however, that London needed time to adjust to the idea of repertory and Frohman's seventeen week season was not long enough to establish the habit.

More important, however, in Archer's view was the lack of a controlling manager at the Duke of York's. Frohman, absent in the United States for much of the planning period and caught up in the promotion of his other theatrical concerns, had failed to supervise the venture. He had taken no control of budgeting or expenditure, nor had he taken any lead in the selection of plays. This he had left entirely to the dramatists, and the result was a programme, interesting enough for the devotees of the 'new drama', but which had taken little account of popular taste. *The Madras House* and *Misalliance* were, in quite different ways, too innovative in their dramatic form ever to have been put in the same short season. *Helena's Path* was too much in the old mould, despite Barker's direction, ever to appeal to a Repertory audience. *The Sentimentalists* was an incomplete and basically a 'non-dramatic' work, that might have attracted a handful of faithfuls at a Stage Society Sunday evening, but could never appeal to a regular audience. Archer hoped that the participants would learn from their mistakes. 'The scant success of the Repertory Theatre will be a disaster indeed if the authors concerned misread its moral and lay the blame on everybody but themselves.'

On a purely practical level, the Duke of York's was not a suitable theatre for the Repertory experiment. It was in the first place too large, with a capacity of 1,094, only slightly smaller than the Savoy which had faced similar problems, and secondly, its backstage facilities were inadequate. There was no storage space so that when sets were struck they had either to be left outside or transported to a warehouse some distance away. At its height the Repertory Theatre was presenting four different plays in the one week. The stage management must have been nightmarish.

All in all, then, the Repertory Theatre at the Duke of York's must be regarded as one of those fruitful failures in which the story of the progress of the 'new drama' abounds. Attention moved, as Barker had predicted, to the provinces in the hope that conditions there might prove to be more favourable.

The Provincial Repertory Movement (1908–1914)

The next home for the 'new drama' was found in the large provincial cities which, having experienced vast commercial and industrial expansion throughout the nineteenth century, were, at the beginning of the twentieth, ready to establish themselves as cultural centres. Repertory Theatres were founded in Manchester in 1907, in Glasgow in 1909 and in Liverpool in 1911. Although the particular circumstances in which each theatre was founded were different, the motivation of the founders and the aims they sought to achieve were markedly similar.

One of the many deleterious effects of the long-run system and the fashion for expensive and elaborate scenery was that the old practice of one star actor touring the provinces alone and playing with the local stock company fell into disuse, and instead an entire London production, sets, costumes, actors and all, went out on the road. The result was that the local companies which had provided the principal training ground for actors gradually went out of business, and the large industrial cities became totally dependent on tours of West End successes for their theatrical entertainment. The demise of the local companies meant that the theatre had lost touch with the community. Both in Glasgow and in Manchester, it was made very clear that one of the reasons for founding a repertory theatre was to free the city from theatrical domination by London. The fare provided by the commercial touring companies was also criticised, for a growing number of people in these cities wanted something more from their theatre than the glossy (or often slightly tarnished) West End successes. A branch of the Independent Theatre Society had been founded in Manchester in 1893, and had introduced Ibsen to the north west in concert hall performances. Glasgow's Stage Society was inaugurated with a lecture from the President of the London Stage Society, Frederick Whelen, in 1908. Granville Barker lectured to the Liverpool Playgoers' Club, founded a year later. The people who belonged to such societies wanted, as their predecessors at the ITS and the Stage Society had done, serious plays with literary merit, well acted and well directed. The Vedrenne–Barker management at the Court became their inspiration and their model. A further aim, sometimes hesitantly and sometimes confidently expressed, was to create a regional school of 'new dramatists'.

The Manchester theatre differed from the other two in that the money to fund it came from an individual benefactor, Miss Annie Horniman, and was not raised by subscriptions from local people. Miss Horniman had financed a season of 'new drama' at the Avenue Theatre in

London in 1894, which included the first performance of Shaw's *Arms and the Man*. She had been most generous in her contributions to the Abbey Theatre in Dublin, providing a theatre and an annual subsidy, but after a quarrel with W.B. Yeats and Lady Gregory, she decided to invest her considerable fortune and her consummate energy in founding a theatre in Manchester. The Manchester Repertory Theatre opened with a performance of *David Ballard* by Charles McEvoy in the Midland Hotel in 1907. The following year the company acquired the Gaiety Theatre, with a capacity of 1,250.

Glasgow Repertory Theatre, likewise, owed its inception to the work of a veteran of the Abbey Theatre, in this case its production manager, Alfred Wareing, but the project was financed initially by £1,000 raised in £1 shares by Glasgow citizens. The said 'citizens' came from the intellectual middle classes as had the majority of the Court audiences. Members of the University of Glasgow, most notably the Professor of English, Macneile Dixon, and the staff of *The Glasgow Herald* were among the most ardent supporters. The Royalty Theatre was leased for a season for £80. Its capacity of 1,314 made it the largest house in the country to be used for repertory. It opened with a production of Shaw's *You Never Can Tell* in April 1909.

The support for the establishment of a repertory theatre in Liverpool came, as it had in Glasgow, from the University, in particular, from Professor Charles Reilly, the founder of the Playgoers' Club and Professor Ramsay Muir, and from the local press. A local journalist, Lascelles Abercrombie, gave invaluable support to the venture. The Liverpool Repertory Theatre, the only one of the three to survive to the present day, was in fact an offshoot of the Manchester company, some of whom came to do a short season in Liverpool. It opened with a production of

Galsworthy's *Strife* in February 1911. Galsworthy was present at the final rehearsals, and William Archer, the supporter of so many 'new drama' ventures, attended the first night.

The repertoire of the three theatres followed very closely the pattern established at the Court and presented plays by the dramatists which the Vedrenne–Barker management had nurtured or discovered. Glasgow presented nine of Shaw's plays including *Man and Superman*, with Barker and Lillah McCarthy in their original parts. *You Never Can Tell* was revived many times by popular plebiscite, and a private performance of the still banned *Mrs Warren's Profession* was given, ostensibly for the Playgoers' League. All three companies staged *Candida*, and Manchester revived Shaw's first play, *Widowers' Houses*. *The Voysey Inheritance* by Barker, St John Hankin's *The Return of the Prodigal* and *The Cassilis Engagement*, Galsworthy's *Strife* and *Justice* and Masefield's *The Tragedy of Nan* were produced by all the repertories. Each company had its favourite 'new dramatist'. Glasgow's audiences preferred Shaw, and Manchester's, Galsworthy, who became almost a 'house' dramatist. Manchester also took up the classical aspect of the Court repertoire with productions of Murray's translations of *Hippolytus* and *The Trojan Women*. The Court tradition of presenting the best of European drama was continued. All the companies performed Ibsen's *An Enemy of the People*, Liverpool and Glasgow produced *A Doll's House*, and Glasgow also attempted the notoriously difficult *Brand*. The first production of a play by Chekhov in Britain was Glasgow Repertory Theatre's presentation of *The Seagull* in 1909, directed by George Calderon.

As far as the creation of a new school of 'new dramatists' was concerned only the Manchester company achieved any real success. Ironically, the seeds of its collapse lay in the critical acclaim won by Stanley Houghton's *Hindle Wakes*, for the play's transfer to London with the best actors of the company meant an inevitable drop in standards of the resident Manchester company. Glasgow tried hard to create a native Scottish drama but the best it achieved was J.J. Bell's *Wee Macgregor*, little more than a music-hall sketch, J.A. Ferguson's one act play, *Campbell of Kilmohr* and *The Price of Coal* by Harold Brighouse, an import from the Manchester company. The production of *The Adder* by Lascelles Abercrombie in Liverpool in 1913 looked as if it might be the beginning of a new wave of provincial 'new drama', but at the outbreak of the First World War, Liverpool's programme which had always included more former West End successes than the other two companies became more orientated towards the commercial reper-toire. With the exception of *Hindle Wakes*, the provincial repertory movement did not make a substantial input to the body of 'new drama'.

The group of actors who worked in the provincial companies, and there tended to be free movement of players around the three theatres, included a great many veterans of the Court, the Savoy and the Repertory Theatre. As one would expect with so many of the actors of the 'new drama' involved in all three provincial companies, the acting was praised for just those features which had distinguished acting at the Court and at the Repertory Theatre, *viz*, the stress on the text and the attempt to interpret as faithfully as possible the author's meaning, the emphasis on playing together as a company rather than as solo performers, the achievement of a balance between naturalistic and stylised playing, and the development of the ability to cope with a wide range of parts. Although the provincial repertories, with the possible exception of Manchester, failed to carry the writing of the 'new drama' forward, they were to prove significant in providing the British theatre with more 'new actors' and replaced the nineteenth-century stock companies as nurseries for talented young people.

Regrettably, only Liverpool was to survive the First World War. Glasgow, under the directorship of Lewis Casson, had recovered from years of deficit and was showing a small profit when war broke out and the theatre was closed. The remaining funds were eventually used to finance the Scottish National Players in the 1920s. Manchester suffered from the commercial success of *Hindle Wakes*, and from the fact that there had never been enough civic involvement in Miss Horniman's enterprise. Liverpool survived by abandoning the avant-garde experiments of its director, Basil Dean, and turning to a policy of presenting such well-proven favourites as T.W. Robertson's *Caste*, and *The Liars* by Henry Arthur Jones. Once again it looked as though theatrically, the 'new drama' had failed. Yet Manchester and Glasgow have remained centres of theatrical activity both professionally and academically. The grandchild of Glasgow Repertory Theatre, the Citizens' Theatre, and the Royal Exchange in Manchester are acknowledged as first rate international companies. The provincial pioneers may not have succeeded in divorcing themselves from London for their dramatic supplies in terms of either acting or playwriting, but at least they were eager to show to their fellow citizens the best of London theatre rather than the bland upholstered drama of the touring companies, and they sowed seeds that were to bear fruit in later years.

Part 2
Playwrights and Plays

1
Harley Granville Barker

Harley Granville Barker was born in London on 25 November 1877. His father made a living by converting houses into flats, and his mother, under the name of Miss Granville, was a professional reciter. As a child, Barker often appeared with her in small halls and assembly rooms. In 1891, he became a pupil at Sarah Thorne's dramatic school in Margate, where he met the actor, Berte Thomas, with whom he collaborated in his early attempts at dramatic writing, *The Family of the Oldroyds*, *The Weather-hen* and *Our Visitor to 'Work-a-Day'*. None is published, and only *The Weather-hen* was ever produced, at a special matinée at Terry's Theatre in June 1899.

In 1892, Barker made his first appearance on the London stage, as the Third Young Man in *The Poet and the Puppets*, a musical by Charles Brookfield, with whom he was later to come into conflict when Brookfield was appointed Examiner of Plays. Little is known of his early work, until he appeared as Romeo with Ben Greet's company in 1895. Juliet was played by Lillah McCarthy, who became one of the leading actresses in the 'new drama', and whom Barker married in 1906.

Although in common with all the actors who pioneered the 'new drama', Barker had to appear in the run-of-the-mill plays in the commercial theatre of the 'nineties, he became increasingly involved with those whose work sought to overthrow its principles. He appeared with William Poel's Elizabethan Stage Society as Richard II in 1899 and took the title role in Marlowe's *Edward II* in 1903. Yet it was in the Stage Society, founded in 1899, that he discovered an ardent body of likeminded actors and writers. It provided him not only with the chance to appear in challenging parts in plays by Ibsen and Shaw, but it also gave him his first opportunity to direct in 1900. His first production was a triple bill of *The House of Usna* by Fiona MacLeod, the pseudonym of William Sharp, and *Interior* and *The Death of Tintagiles*, by Maeterlinck. In 1902, he directed for the Society his own play, *The Marrying of Ann Leete*. Barker became associated with the leading figures in the 'new drama' movement in which he himself was to play a major role. He provided the movement with a permanent home at the Court Theatre in 1904 and devoted the next ten years of his life to raising the standard of acting, writing and directing in the British theatre, at the Court, the Savoy and the Duke of York's, and later, for short seasons, in association with his wife, Lillah McCarthy, at the Little Theatre, at the St James's Theatre, and at the Kingsway.

Between 1904 and 1911 Barker wrote his three finest plays, *The Voysey Inheritance* (Court, 1905), *Waste* (privately performed by the Stage Society, 1907) and *The Madras House* (Duke of York's, 1909). In 1912 he first turned his attention to directing Shakespeare's plays, with a production of *The Winter's Tale* at the Savoy. This was followed by *Twelfth Night* in the same year and by *A Midsummer Night's Dream* in 1914.

These three brilliant and revolutionary productions sadly marked the end of Barker's career on the English stage. In 1915, while directing a season of plays in New York, he met and fell in love with Helen Huntington, a wealthy writer. On his return to Britain, he enlisted in the Royal Horse Artillery, but by 1917, he was back in America to give a series of lectures. He and Lillah McCarthy were divorced in April of that year, and within fourteen months he married Helen Huntington. His second wife disliked the stage in general and Shaw (and his politics) in particular. Barker assisted on a few productions, *Waste*, with Michael Mac Owan (1936) and *King Lear*, with Lewis Casson (1940), but he virtually abandoned practical work in the theatre and turned his attention to writing.

He wrote two more plays, *The Secret Life* (1923) and *His Majesty* (1928). These were not produced, and although they do contain some flashes of the old genius, are vastly inferior to his earlier work. In collaboration with his second wife, he translated, from the Spanish, plays by Gregorio Sierra and Serafin and Joaquin Quintero. Additionally, he collected the ideas and experiences he had had in his practical theatrical career in the publication of *The Exemplary Theatre* (1922), *On Dramatic Method*, the Clerk Lectures at Trinity College, Cambridge (1930), and *The Use of the Drama* (1945). After leaving the theatre, however, his most useful contribution was his *Prefaces to Shakespeare* (the first series was published in 1927) which, in stressing the inherent theatricality in the plays, challenged contemporary literary criticism and the prevailing notions of the primacy of the text as a piece of literature rather than as the raw material for theatrical presentation.

Barker died in Paris, where he had his home for some years, in 1946.

Geoffrey Whitworth called Barker, 'the chief protagonist in that revolution in the theatre which was already astir in the eighteen-nineties, and in full blast from 1900 right up to the outbreak of the first World War'.[1] Even at his first entry to those revolutionary circles he was recognised as one of its potential leaders. Shaw called him 'the most distinguished and incomparably the most cultivated person whom circumstances had driven into the theatre at that time'.[2] There were many who felt that his departure from the practical world of theatre left the new movement without a director sensitive to its aims and objectives, and would agree with Bridges–Adam's description of Barker as 'the Lost Leader'.

The Marrying of Ann Leete

The Marrying of Ann Leete was written in 1899, when Barker was 22. It has had two productions, the first by the Stage Society at the Royalty Theatre in London on 26 and 27 January 1902, the second by the Royal Shakespeare Company at the Aldwych in the autumn of 1975.

The theatrically sophisticated audience of the Stage Society found the play 'clever' and 'promising', but 'lacking in almost every dramatic gift including intelligibility'. Although it was precisely the kind of original and unconventional piece that the Society had been founded to produce, and although it was thought to have been very well acted, the consensus was that it was gratuitously mystifying. Even William Archer thought it 'incomprehensible', and his colleague, A.B. Walkley pronounced it 'a practical joke . . . with no trace of constructive talent, no coherence, no clearness'.

The critics of the 1970s thought similarly, and drew on later playwrights' work to solve the enigma. The play was found to be 'a positive lucky dip of apparent influences, several of which Granville Barker cannot in fact have felt'. (J.W. Lambert, *Sunday Times*, 21 September 1975). The investigation of relationship between a high-born woman and a working-class man reminded reviewers of Strindberg's *Miss Julie* and of D.H. Lawrence's novel, *Lady Chatterley's Lover*. The picture of the passing of an effete and decadent society was seen, particularly in its creation of atmosphere and ambience, as similar to Chekhov's *The Cherry Orchard* or to Shaw's *Heartbreak House*. The dialogue, employing half-finished sentences and pauses and carefully placed verbal echoes, was thought to be Pinteresque. The implication is that Barker, in prefiguring the works of later writers, had written a startlingly innovative piece that in language, structure and subject matter was a significant advance on the drama of the turn of the century. But he was also drawing on several contemporary influences; on melodrama – the *Athenaeum* critic (1 February 1902) called the play 'a burlesque of the *Lady of Lyons*, – on naturalism, in that, on the surface at any rate, characters talk and act in a manner that reflects the real world, and on symbolism, for Barker, more crudely in this piece than in his later work, employs a battery of symbols to express his deeper meaning. The delicate picture of an upper-class society in decline was reminiscent of the work of George Meredith, whose *Essay on Comedy* had been published in 1898.

For a play with such a reputation for being 'difficult' the plot is simple. It is set in the late eighteenth century at Markswayde, the home of the Leete family. Carnaby Leete, a brilliantly devious politician, has three children. His elder daughter, Sarah, has been married for some time to Lord Cottesham, a powerful Tory minister, a marriage arranged to assist her father's transition from the Whig to the Tory party. Although the political end was achieved, neither Sarah nor her husband has found satisfaction in their union. George Leete, Carnaby's son, has married Dolly Crowe, the daughter of a local farmer, a match despised by his father. The youngest child, Ann, remains, and it is on her 'marrying' that the play centres.

Carnaby, having successfully manipulated a change of party through the marrying of one daughter, now seeks to effect an expedient return to the Whigs, by giving Ann to a pillar of the opposition, Lord John Carp. The idea first occurs to him when Lord John, in order to win a bet that Ann cannot cross the dark garden without screaming, kisses her. Her resulting scream, in the dark, is an effective opening for the play. Lord John at once apologises. He, like Ann, realises that he has broken the rules of the game, but Leete, seizing the opportunity with cynical pragmatism, arranges first of all a duel with Carp, and then his marriage to Ann. The 'stolen' kiss, Ann regards as a violation of herself, but it also awakens her sexuality. She, in fact, returns it, and, in her bewilderment and confusion, she at first appears to agree to the union, although she demands instruction as to the rules of the new game she is to play. The example, on the one hand, of the collapse of Sarah's 'political' marriage resulting in the deterioration of her personality into superficially witty cynicism and, on the other, the birth of twins to her low-bred sister-in-law, force Ann to come to a decision on her own future that is at odds with her father's plan to use her for his personal advancement. She proposes marriage to the gardener, John Abud, who has been seen tending the garden where the Leetes and their associates plot and play. After a wedding breakfast, described by critics as Hogarthian in its grotesque satire of eighteenth-century characters, the couple depart to walk nine miles through the snow to Abud's cottage. Markswayde is 'to let' and the era of the Leetes is over.

Although the story is a simple one, Barker does not choose to tell it in a straightforward narrative. There is virtually no exposition, and the audience is required to pick up such relevant information as it can from the allusive dialogue. On the surface it seems to resemble the language of casual conversation, but this is used more often to conceal than to reveal the thoughts and feelings of the characters. As they play games with their lives, they play games with their words, and the spectator, like Ann, must dig deep to discover the rules.

The theme of the play is not a difficult one to grasp. As in *The Voysey Inheritance* and *The Madras House*, Barker shows the passing of an old order of civilisation and the emergence of a new force that is young, strong and vital. The characters belonging to the former are cautious, wary and afraid of taking risks. The regenerators, like Ann, are not 'careful with their lives', a phrase which echoes Ibsen's Button-moulder in *Peer Gynt*, 'To be oneself is to kill oneself', itself a paraphrase of St Matthew, 'Whosoever will save his life shall lose it'. The plays show the often painful process of transition, and it was because the late eighteenth century, like the late nineteenth, was just such a time of transition that *Ann Leete* was set in this period.

In a long note attached to Barker's copy of the play, now in the British Library, he expands on his decision to place the piece in the previous century in terms of costume and hairdressing.

> The period seems to have been in costume as well as in manners a transitional one, one in which not only a man's nature, but his opinions were very much known by the fashions he followed. The greatest tendency of course was from the ornate to the simple; silks and satins were going out, and the rougher, more sober-looking materials coming in.

The wearing of wigs by Sir George Leete, Carnaby and the two clergymen denote them as being of the 'old order'.

Lord John Carp is fashionable, his hair long and tied back. George has his hair unpowdered and untied. With his marriage to Dolly Crowe he has stepped out of the smart world and is, as Sarah describes him, 'a cork, trying to sink socially'. Farmer Crowe, the new tenant of Markswayde, has his own hair, close cropped. The characters' physical appearance is used to align them in relation to the theme.

The characters belonging to the 'old order' are not only defined by their fashions in dress but by the setting they inhabit. The first three acts which adhere to the Unities of Time and of Place are set in the garden of Markswayde, formal and elegant, but a Waste Land. There has been no rain for weeks, the cracked nymph of the fountain pours no water, the pool below is stagnant, the grass is bare, and the heavy overblown roses are ready to snap under their own weight. No landscape is visible and the characters are kept firmly in this patterned decaying enclosure from just before dawn till evening. Abud, who is seen unobtrusively tending the garden throughout, is consulted at noon as to when the rain will come, as though he were some kind of divining prophet:

> DR REMNANT: Will it rain before nightfall?
> BUD: About then, sir, I should say.
> CARNABY: Oh this cracked earth. Will it rain . . .
> Will it rain?

The rain comes for Carnaby in the late evening as Ann refuses to marry Lord John Carp, with the words, 'I refuse to be tempted.' As the mystified Sarah, who insists that it is not raining, asks Ann, 'What is to become of you?' Ann proposes to Abud. The fruitfulness of their union is prefigured in the life-giving rain falling on dry earth. Carnaby, fainting, asks to be taken into the house, but not out of the 'pellucid' rain. He is carried in by Abud, whom he addresses as 'son-in-law'. The dying king, his political manipulations and ambitions over, exits, as Ann comments, 'Such a long day it has been . . . now ending.'

The end of the long dry day and the moving of the dramatic action from the claustrophobic garden signify the passing of the 'old order'. The inhabitants of the garden, with the exception of Ann and Abud, belong to a dying breed. 'How lively one feels, and isn't', says Sarah, in Act I. 'What ghosts we are', murmurs George in reply. Although Carnaby in his patterned wilderness claims that he is 'as a green bay tree', the realistic Lord John moments later says, 'Your father is past his prime.'

The talk in the first three acts is all of 'gaming' and 'play', an apt metaphor for political intrigue. As Lord John puts it, 'Politics is a game for clever children, women and fools.' Lord John kisses Ann, not out of affection or sexual attraction, but to win a mare from the stables of a neighbour, Mr Tatton, who has been playing whist with the company inside the house. George cannot see the cards in the dark garden, but the increasing light shows that Tatton has the King, and Carnaby, the arch-manipulator, the Ace, in the game that was interrupted by Ann's scream. Sarah exclaims, 'Who doesn't love sport?' but Tatton, upset that Carp is both gamester and umpire, bemoans his own folly in playing two games at once. Carnaby, fired by the idea of linking himself with both political parties by marriage, or as he puts it 'having an anchor in each camp', relishes the notion of 'tickling the Carp'. He sees politics as sport not as public service. When Sarah is exiled to Yorkshire by her estranged husband, 'cards' are banned, although she confesses to be 'a little fond of play'. She is condemned to a life of patience and chess problems. Political 'gambling' is a way of life for Carnaby Leete, and his elder daughter has become the pawn in the game of chance. Barker's attraction to the political world was to be seen again in *Waste*. He remained interested in the struggles for power, the intrigue, and the manipulation of human beings by their fellows in the pursuit of dominance.

The first three acts, despite a rambling dramatic structure, are held together by recurring imagery and by a classical use of Time and Place. The fourth act is set sometime later, in winter, inside Markswayde, and we witness the final death throes of its inhabitants. Barker introduces six new characters; the Leete grandparents, he, an old-fashioned snob, she, a querulous and demanding hypochondriac; Lady Leete's drunken chaplain, Tozer, embodies the death of spiritual values in such a world; Farmer Crowe, George Leete's father-in-law, and his wife, Dolly, are vulgar and money grubbing; Mr Prestige, Abud's uncle, is, as shown by his name, every bit as proud of his family's entry into the gentry as Crowe, although his expression of his delight is rather more discreet.

These characters are nicely drawn caricatures and interesting parts for actors. They have a minimal function in extending the audience's experience of the corruption inherent in the old world, but the fourth act, in terms of the expression of the theme of the play and of furthering the progress of the narrative, is totally redundant and immaturely profligate of dramatic resources.

There is one very good scene, between Sarah and her former lover, Lord John's brother, Lord Arthur Carp. Because of interruptions first by Dimmuck, the butler, and later by Mrs Opie, the governess, the pair are forced to repeat their very formal approach to each other, and the repetition epitomises both the mechanical and the obsessively secretive nature of the relationship that the world of intrigue forces upon the men and women who seek to play its game. It is also made clear that Sarah refused to leave her husband for Lord Arthur, whom she plainly loved, largely on the grounds that he could not provide for her adequately:

> LORD ARTHUR: . . . It was my little home in the country somehow said aloud you didn't care for me.

Sarah, unlike Ann, is incapable of leaving the dying world of her own free will and becomes an outcast, expelled from both the 'old order' and the 'new'. But she is intelligent enough to recognise the flaw that brought down the House of Leete:

> SARAH: If we . . . this house I'm speaking of . . . had made friends where we've only made tools and fools we shouldn't now be cursed as we are . . . all.

In their farewells to Ann after the wedding celebrations as she leaves the dying House of Leete, both Sarah and Carnaby recognise the symbolic significance of her departure, the severance of her connections with the old order. Carnaby's words, 'I can do without you', appear harsh, but the stage direction reads '*Quietly, as he kisses her cheek*'. The gesture and the tone, if not the words, are those of a benediction. Sarah's whispered, 'Forget us', is in the same vein. They rejoice in her bid for freedom from their decadent environment. 'There', concludes Carnaby, 'has started the new century.'

The final scene in the small cottage is a coda to the main action. The stage space is reduced, the humble cottage being in marked contrast to the formal garden of the first three acts and the ornate lavishness of the interior of Markswayde. The new order is still embryonic and tentative. Like the hyacinths that Abud offers to his new wife, it has still to come to full bloom.

Ann's motivation for rejecting the dying world of the Leetes is twofold. First, she has before her the example of her sister's unhappiness and her rejection when events prove her to be no longer of material benefit to her husband and to her father. Sarah 'worked her best for her family', and even in the face of her own exile, pleads with her ex-lover to 'be useful' to her father. Ann sees that Sarah's involvement in the old world has not only made her life miserable, but has actually corrupted her former values. It is the evil in Sarah that Ann rejects in her denunciation of her sister:

> ANN: And I curse you . . . because, we being sisters, I suppose I am much what you were, about to be married; and I think, Sally, you'd have cursed your present self. I could become all that you are and more . . . but I didn't choose.

Ann's statement 'I could become all that you are and more', belies Irving Wardle's criticism of Barker's representation of her character in his *Times* review (19 September 1975). Wardle claims that 'Ann emerges more as a means of revealing surrounding characters than a source of interest in herself', that she is 'denied access to the sub-text of the play' and is, in her ignorance of the basic rules of the society in which she has been reared, unrealistically naïve. Ann's veneer of naïvete is itself a political statement. Her marriage to Abud is as much a marriage of convenience as her marriage to Carp would have been. But it is a marriage for her convenience, not for her father's. She is determined to begin again, for herself:

ANN: Papa . . . I said . . . we've all been in too great a
hurry getting civilised. False dawn. I mean to go back.

The 'false dawn' for Ann was the kiss in the dark garden,
false, in that it was a Judas kiss of treachery and cheating,
but a 'dawn' too, in that it awakened her sexuality, and in so
doing inadvertently offered her an opportunity for escape.
She becomes capable of seeing John Abud, not as a mere
servant, but as a man, 'straight-limbed and clear-eyed . . .
and I'm a woman'. She 'goes back' and, indeed, forward in
her proposal to him. Abud is dumbfounded, but Ann
manipulates him with all the cunning to the Leetes:

ANN: If we two were alone here in this garden and
everyone else in the world were dead . . . what would
you answer?
ABUD (*still amazed*): Why . . . yes.

Ann's question raises a complex set of references. 'Two
alone in a garden' has, of course, connotations of Eden,
and the gardener, Abud, is almost too easy a prey for this
sophisticated Eve. The others in their world, Carnaby,
Sarah, George and Carp are 'dead', ghosts in the garden, as
George described them in Act I. The question is phrased in
such a way that the desired response is elicited. Ann, who
has played the innocent, demonstrates her political acu-
men. One must believe her assertion to Sarah, 'I could
become all that you are and more'.

If Lord John Carp has made Ann aware of her womanhood, it is Abud who makes her conscious of what Shaw
was later to call the 'Life-Force' within her. When news is
brought of the birth of twins to George's wife, Dolly, whom
Abud had previously courted, he is full of joy:

ABUD (*in an ecstasy*): This is good. Oh, Dolly and God
    . . . This is good.
ANN (*round-eyed*): I wonder that you can be pleased.
ABUD (*apologising . . . without apology*): It's life.
ANN (*struck*): Yes, it is.

Carnaby Leete finds such fecundity vulgar, and refuses to
allow the children to be christened with family names. As
his son leaves to visit his newborn babies, Carnaby bitterly
disowns him. 'The begetting of you, sir, was a waste of
time.' For the Leetes, children are for the use of their
parents. If they cease to be useful they are rejected, like
George and Sarah, or 'let go' as Ann describes it.

Carnaby's attitude is in stark contrast to Abud's heartfelt
exhilaration in the fact of birth, an emotion that infects Ann
and motivates her subsequent actions. As in other examples of the 'new drama', including Barker's own plays
Waste and *The Madras House*, the liberation of the woman
as an independent agent is closely linked to her willingness
to bear children. Like Shaw, he somewhat ambiguously
links the 'new woman', an independent self-sufficient being
with the concept of procreation. George says to Ann, 'You
want a new world . . . you new women', but Ann is not a
'new woman' in the sense that Nora is in *A Doll's House*,
nor Mrs Alving in *Ghosts*, nor even Hedda Gabler. She is
more a symbol of rebirth than an assertion of individual
female identity. Her 'new world' is that of domesticity and
procreation.

Abud, in the final scene, asserts his mastery. His wife
must rise early, provide a dinner for the field and have a hot
meal ready in the evening. She must mop the brick floor, as
his mother did before her, and he must never be reminded
of her highborn ancestors. Ann Leete may have won her
freedom from the premature civilisation of her family and

the 'false dawn' of fine manners and sophisticated society, but her new life is not romanticised. She shrinks from Abud's offering of hyacinths, as she does from the kiss which he claims as his right. It may be that the kiss reminds her of the stolen embrace from Lord John Carp in the garden that began the play. As she meditates on and rationalises her state, Abud's comments are prosaic and practical. One is led to question the viability of this union, although not the courage of each contractor. They are not being 'careful of their lives', but if their marriage is to succeed it is first, because they will work together, secondly, because they will become parents, and thirdly, because they will never admit that it has failed. Abud's candle as he lights Ann up the stairs – a contrast to the unlit candelabra borne by George in Act I – is a symbol of such hope, and in theatrical terms, perhaps has more impact than the strained dialogue of the alien couple in the cold cottage.

Barker's first published play is the work of an immature dramatist, but it establishes the themes and the techniques that he was to develop in his later work – the fascination with political intrigue, the marriage of naturalistic detail with symbolic or metaphysical significance, the challenge to the established order by young people of courage and vision, the use of everyday speech to convey a philosophical subtext and the sensitive investigation of personal and social codes of morality.

The Voysey Inheritance

The Voysey Inheritance, Barker's best-known play, was first performed at the Court Theatre in November 1905, and was most recently revived as a television production in 1978. It is a much more compact and comprehensible play than *The Marrying of Ann Leete*. William Archer, who had previously been frustrated by the fact that Barker's un-doubted dramatic promise was negated by his seemingly wilful obscurity, called it 'a play conceived and composed with original mastery'. It is a superb example of the 'new drama', in the critical view of the capitalist system which it presents, in its naturalistic picture of an upper middle-class family in the Edwardian era, and in its close examination of accepted social conventions and their impact on individual moral decisions. This play owes more to the influence of Ibsen and of Shaw than does any other piece by Barker. The whole concept of 'inheritance' is reminiscent of Ibsen, in that in employing the Norwegian dramatist's retrospec-tive technique (i.e., the 'action' that motivates the drama has taken place before the play itself begins), Barker investigates the way in which the sins of the father are visited on the son. *The Voysey Inheritance* is also reminis-cent of Shaw's *Widowers' Houses* and *Mrs Warren's Profession*, in which a child is forced to confront the fact that his education, his upbringing and his comfortable lifestyle have all been financed by resources acquired by very dubious means. The moral principles of a young idealist are challenged when he is forced to shoulder the inescapable burden of his parent's past misdemeanours.

Like its predecessor, *The Marrying of Ann Leete*, and its successor, *The Madras House, The Voysey Inheritance* concerns a family, a 'House', as in the classical Greek tragedies, and one that faces a crisis in its affairs. Mr Voysey is a prosperous solicitor, a pillar of upper-middle-class society, with a house in Chislehurst in Kent and a flourishing legal practice. He has four sons, Trenchard, a lawyer from whom he has been estranged for some time, Booth, a former army officer, Hugh, an artist, and Edward, who has followed his father into the family business. There are two daughters, Honor, who is unmarried and who serves the family domestically as Edward is expected to serve it professionally, and Ethel, who is about to be married. Early in the first act, Mr Voysey explains to Edward that for many years he has been guilty of handling his clients' money in a fraudulent manner. Although continuing to pay them interest at the correct rate, he and his family have been living off the investors' capital. Edward's first reaction is one of horror and disgust, although he is somewhat mollified when his father explains that he inherited the problem from Edward's grandfather and began his illegal malpractice by trying to put things right. In fact, it emerges later that Mr Voysey had succeeded in putting the firm on a stable footing but, intoxicated by the gambling instinct, he had continued his speculations long after they were necessary. On Mr Voysey's death, between Acts II and III, Edward falls heir to the firm and to the fraud. The play is primarily concerned with how he deals with his inheritance.

At the outset, Edward is an idealist, whose ideals have never been challenged:

> MR VOYSEY: My dear Edward, you've lived a quiet humdrum life up to now, with your poetry and your sociology and your agnosticism and your ethics of this and your ethics of that . . . and you've never been brought face to face with any really vital question.

Alice Maitland, a family friend who has refused Edward's 'four and a half' proposals of marriage, calls him 'a perfect little pocket-guide to life'. His brother Hugh's wife, Beatrice, regards him at the outset as 'a well-principled prig'.

Edward is forced, through his acceptance of his inheritance, to test his principles. His initial reaction is to preserve his personal integrity at all costs. 'I can't meddle in it', he says, with distaste. He then wants 'to do the honest thing', confess his father's crimes and pay back as much money as possible to all the creditors by relinquishing his own and his family's assets. He comes to realise, however, partly through the influence of Alice Maitland, that this course of action would be foolish and impractical, benefiting neither the creditors nor himself. His responsibility to the firm's clients is more complex and ultimately more important than the preservation of his own ethical code, and more important than adhering to the strict letter of the law. He learns that his hitherto inviolate set of principles must be tested if they are to be of any value. As he admits in Act IV, 'I had to prove what my honesty was worth . . . what I was worth.' The concepts of 'right' and 'wrong', 'legal' and 'illegal' are explored throughout the play. In response to the simple statement by Edward, 'It's not right', Mr Voysey replies, 'That is a word, Edward, which one should learn to use very carefully. You mean that from time to time I have had to go beyond the letter of the law.'

This theme is echoed in the exchange between Edward and his brother, Hugh, after Edward has told his family of their father's criminal activity:

EDWARD: It's strange that people will believe you can do right by means which they know to be wrong.

HUGH: (*taking great interest in this*) Come, what do we know about right and wrong? Let's say legal and illegal. You're so down on the governor because he has trespassed against the etiquette of your own profession.

In order to do 'right', i.e., to try to compensate his clients and in addition to protect his father's good name, Edward is forced to act illegally, indeed to abandon his uncritical acceptance of the legal system, a fact which he finds difficult to accept, and a practice against which his whole being revolts.

The letter of the Law is embodied in Trenchard Voysey, the eldest son of the family, who has quarrelled with his father many years previously. The reasons for the breach are left ambiguous. It is hinted that Trenchard had suspected his father of fraudulent dealings, but more important is the implication, barely stated, that the two were temperamentally incompatible. Mr Voysey is, to use Ibsen's term, a man with 'a robust conscience'. Trenchard has handed his conscience over to the legal system. He makes only a brief appearance in the play, at his father's funeral. The introduction of the secondary character of Trenchard might be seen as an attempt by Barker to establish an appropriate *milieu* for his main characters, and imply that he is being as prodigal of acting resources here as he was in the wedding scene in Act IV of *The Marrying of Ann Leete*. Yet, even in this, his most orthodox play in terms of its adherence to the principles of Naturalism, he transcends Naturalism, in that Trenchard's response to Edward's revelation that the House of Voysey is built on fraud is not only that of an individual. Trenchard also has the dramatic function of personifying the correct *legal* response to the problem. Edward at this stage in his development feels that ethically each member of the family should return all his or her money to the firm in order to pay off as many debts as possible. Trenchard disagrees:

TRENCHARD: The family is not called upon to beggar itself in order to pay back to every client to whom Father owed a pound perhaps eight shillings instead of seven.

The Law may be entitled to its pound of flesh, but not to a drop of blood shed for sentimental reasons. He appreciates Edward's difficulty, but significantly offers him only 'professional' help. Trenchard remains safe within the Law, just as Edward's other brothers remain safe within the accepted conventions of conservative upper-middle-class manners, or of artistic idealism.

Major Booth Voysey casts himself in the role of the upholder of the Family honour. Edward's revelation of their father's swindling highlights his attitude, 'I may be right or I may be wrong . . . I am feeling far less concerned about the clients' money than I am at the terrible blow to the Family which this exposure will strike. Money, after all, can to a certain extent be done without . . . but honour . . .'. Booth is quite clear in his own mind about right and wrong. 'Right', for him is what preserves the veneer of upper middle-class comfort and stability. 'Wrong' is what threatens it. To be honourable is to be thought honourable, just as to Mr Voysey, to be rich was to be seen to be rich. As far as Booth is concerned, the financial skulduggery may continue just as long as it is never revealed. Likewise, in his opinion, Hugh and Beatrice must continue in their unhappy marriage to avoid any scandal. In trying to bring about a reconciliation, or rather bullying them into staying together, Booth incites, first, the tenets of religion ('Surely, as a woman, Beatrice, the religious point of it ought to appeal to you'), then the Law, and finally 'the Family'. In the face of so many 'authorities', he finds it hard to believe that the couple can persist in their rational decision to part. A tirade against the Family and its suffocating 'comfort' is the only response from Hugh, who, unlike Edward, has not had to face a moral crisis. As his wife puts it, 'Hugh's tragedy is that he is just clever enough to have found himself out, and no cleverer.' He recognises that his art is as fraudulent as his father's speculations, but can do nothing about it. He is left at the end of the play in the same stage of moral development in which Edward was at the beginning, in possession of a fine set of principles that cannot be translated into action.

It would be wrong, however, to imply that each of the brothers is a crudely drawn personification of attitudes, Trenchard of the Law, Booth of Upper-Middle-Class comfort and Hugh of Art. Each one is a personality as well as a personification. Booth's offer to come into the office to help Edward may be comic, but it is sincere. Hugh, despite his rhetoric opposing Voysey materialism, tries to borrow money in a revealing little encounter with his brother in Act IV. In addition, they all seem to belong to the same family, treating each other with a recognisable mixture of familiarity and distance. Barker stresses the similarity, even between the most dissimilar sons. '*Trenchard and Hugh . . . are as unlike each other as it is possible for Voyseys to be, but that isn't very unalike.*' All the sons have a tendency to hold conversations by delivering rhetorical speeches, and all except Trenchard return regularly to the family home, despite expressing from time to time a reluctance to do so. The Voyseys belong together, and Barker's skill enables him to create a believable group of characters whose personalities at the same time illustrate the theme of the play, the search for an independent moral code untrammelled by received notions of religious, legal or social attitudes.

Edward alone puts aside his 'pocket guide to life' and faces with an independent and courageous mind the task of restoring honour to the Voysey inheritance. Ironically, it is he who most successfully follows his father's advice, 'You have to cultivate your own sense of right and wrong . . . deal your own justice.' Edward learns the lesson Ibsen preached in *The Master Builder*, one that the elder Voysey had fully assimilated, 'You must consult your own conscience and decide on your own course of action.' Edward's jettisoning of all the rule-books, those of religion and of the Law, give him the stature to save something from the House of Voysey, as Ann's repudiation of the rules of political gamesmanship enable her to bring new vitality to the decaying Leetes.

Desmond MacCarthy, who reviewed the first production of the play most sympathetically, found the ending unsatisfactory because the audience is not informed as to whether or not Edward is to be prosecuted for his violation of legal ethics. MacCarthy saw this as an example of 'open-endedness', the desire to suggest a continuing life beyond the final curtain, that typified much of the work of the 'new dramatists'. The play is over for Barker when Edward has solved his personal problem, when he has accepted that he alone is morally responsible for his own decisions and actions, and that he cannot take refuge in the accepted codes of values promulgated by certain social institutions. The playwright has chosen to trace the evolution of one man from moral adolescence to moral maturity rather than to mount a full-scale onslaught on the capitalist system.

Edward is no Marxist revolutionary. He never criticises the monetary system nor the distribution of wealth as it exists. He 'shakes his head' when Alice Maitland explains the views of her guardian, 'a person of great character and no principles'. 'You've no moral right to your money . . . you've not earned it or deserved it in any way. So don't be either surprised or annoyed when any enterprising person tries to get it from you. He has at least as much moral right to it as you . . . if he can use it better perhaps he has more.' Edward may choose to treat such Shavian paradoxes with the dismissive attitude he thinks they deserve, but the sentiments which Alice expresses are not dissimilar to those of the elder Voysey. A further paradox is that this 'pillar of society' has been steadily undermining the principles on which that society is based by his financial manipulations.

The Voysey Inheritance may not be such an overt attack on the capitalist system as Shaw mounted in his early plays, but there lies only just beneath the surface the idea that the whole business of investment and interest and of living on the proceeds of unearned income is a suspect game, by its very nature closely linked to gambling. Politics and gambling were similarly linked by the imagery in *The Marrying of Ann Leete*. The fraudulent practices of the elder Voysey, who has much in common with Carnaby Leete, not least in his willingness to use his children to further his own ends, are seen to differ in degree rather than in kind from the dealings of more 'honest' solicitors and stockbrokers. The chief victim of Mr Voysey's 'gambling' is George Booth, an old friend of the family. Although it is never stated explicitly, George Booth is the embodiment of the capitalist ethic. He boasts in Act II, 'I inherited a modest fortune. I have not needed to take the bread out of other men's mouths by working. My money has been wisely administered . . . well, ask your father about that . . . and has . . . not diminished.' Mr Voysey charges him with being 'an old gambler', but Booth maintains, with obvious double meaning for the audience, 'but one ought to see that one's money's put to good use'. It is his desire to withdraw his money from the firm, because he cannot place the same trust in Edward as he did in his father (a nice ironic twist), that finally brings Edward face to face with exposure. For George Booth, the debate over right and wrong which has tortured Edward throughout the play does not exist. He marches out of the office, with the words 'I shall do the right thing, sir . . . never fear.' The 'right thing' is 'the legal thing', as he sees it. 'And I don't see that one is called upon to forgive crimes . . . or why does the law exist?' Both he and the Vicar, another of Voysey's cheated clients, finally agree to withhold prosecution indefinitely, provided that Edward works to settle their accounts first. This selfishness inspires in Edward an anger of which at the beginning of the play one would not have believed him capable. 'Oh, you Christian gentlemen!' he cries, and tells George Booth to 'Go to the devil.' At this point, Edward's sister, Honor, knocks to inquire, 'Am I interrupting business?' The reply demonstrates yet again the marriage of naturalism and metaphor in the play:

> EDWARD: (*Mirthlessly joking*). No. Business is over . . . quite over. Come in, Honor.

Peacey, the head clerk, is another parasite on the capitalist system, for he is able to exist because of the gambling (or thieving, or swindling) of Mr Voysey, who has paid his father and himself 'hush-money', as Edward insists on calling it, for many years. Edward terminates the payments. 'In fact, we no longer make illicit profits out of our clients. So there are none for you to share.' He makes it clear that since he no longer receives 'stolen goods', he is justified in condemning Peacey for having done so. The threat of blackmail is meaningless to Edward since exposure would be welcome. Peacey remains dogged.

> EDWARD: Would you rather I told you plainly what I think of you?
> PEACEY: That I'm a thief because I've taken money from a thief.
> EDWARD: Worse! You're content to have others steal for you.

PEACEY: And who isn't?

Here is the obvious implication, already hinted at by Alice, and boldly stated in Shaw's early works, that the 'receivers' in the Capitalist structure neither know, nor in most cases care, about the source of their dividends and are therefore as guilty as those who exploit others on their behalf. As Margery Morgan has pointed out, Peacey and George Booth are linked thematically and structurally, in that their scenes with Edward open and close the fourth act, and both pose a threat to him. The first scene prefigures the second and prepares us for Edward's reaction to Booth.

While the morality or otherwise of 'the Law' and 'Capitalism' form the main through-lines of the play, Barker also links with those an exploration of contemporary religious attitudes, and in addition, touches on the social roles of women, a theme that was to exercise him more fully in *The Madras House*.

Edward is an avowed agnostic at the outset, but the growing disgust he feels for the practising Christians is evident by the end of the play. The older generation, Mr Voysey, George Booth and Colpus, have successfully organised their lives into separate compartments. Business has nothing to do with pleasure, religion with work, nor family with clients. Mr Voysey advises Edward, 'You must learn, whatever the business may be, to leave it behind you at the office.' In Act II, George Booth echoes this, 'Work on week-days . . . church on Sundays', and Mr Voysey reinforces the argument, 'You must realise that money-making is one thing, and religion another, and family life a third.' It is small wonder then that the fresco for the church designed by Hugh, initially intended to include portraits of local people as the Apostles, caused such a furore. 'The butcher, the plumber and old Sandford' have in the eyes of

Voysey, Colpus and George Booth absolutely nothing to do with the Church. 'We are not fifteenth-century Florentines.' Mr Colpus, like Tozer before him, enjoys his port with sensual relish. He, like George Booth, is involved in the usury of Voysey capitalism. He advises against the prosecution of Edward because he realises that he personally would be no better off with Edward in jail. With his 'excellent head for business,' he can easily separate his faith and his money.

> MR GEORGE BOOTH: He [Mr Colpus] has resolved that during this season of peace and goodwill, he must put the matter from him if he can. But once Christmas is over . . . (*He envisages the old vicar giving Edward a hell of a time then.*)

Although *The Voysey Inheritance* does not deal in great detail with the role of women in society, Mrs Voysey, Emily, Honor, Beatrice, and Ethel contribute to the 'family' atmosphere and, in addition, reflect the different parts in which women are conventionally cast. Mrs Voysey, whose deafness is the source of some comedy, has become aware of her husband's dubious business ethics, but, of course, has never discussed them with him. Perhaps she did not want to hear? She regards this state of affairs as natural, just as she is surprised to read in *Notes and Queries* that Oliver Cromwell, a man of good family, should have done what she regards as dreadful deeds. What she says of the family of Cromwell could apply equally well to the Voyseys, 'It's difficult to discover where the taint crept in.'

Honor Voysey, the spinster daughter, whose naming is not without a certain irony, exemplifies the fate of single women who stay at home. Although Booth maintains, 'Honor leads a useful life – and a happy one. We all love her', Hugh is much more aware of the fact that the Family's exploitation of her 'usefulness' has all but obliterated her personality, 'Yes . . . and what have we always called her? Mother's right hand! I wonder they bothered to give her a name.' As Barker puts it in the stage directions, '*In a less humane society she would have been exposed at birth*'. But Honor does not display any signs of the frustration of the Huxtables in *The Madras House*, and the Family does love her in its own way. She is, after all, necessary to their comfort. An interesting light is thrown on Mr Voysey's character as he sharply reprimands Booth for his rude treatment of Honor over the missing box of cigars.

> MR VOYSEY: Look for your cigars yourself. Honor, go back to your reading or your sewing or whatever you were fiddling at, and fiddle in peace.

With the exception of Hugh's wife, Beatrice, the Voysey women accept the roles that society dictates with little demur. Emily can manage the booming Major by letting him talk himself out, 'But I like him to get his own way as much as possible . . . or think he's getting it. Otherwise he becomes so depressed.' Ethel, the youngest child, and the least inhibited, because by the time she was born 'they were tired of training children', makes a very brief appearance in Act II. She exploits her personal charms and her father's fondness for her for material gain. In the course of the play we hear of her marriage, and her death in childbirth is hinted at. She is important not just because Mr Voysey's indulgent treatment of her shows him in a gentle light – like Carnaby Leete, he is no black-hearted villain – but because she is one of the characters who provide a context for the Voysey household. Most of them do not even appear on stage, such as Mrs Colpus, the Vicar's ailing wife who did not like Mr Voysey, Mrs Pettifer, who is 'looking old' because she is 'getting old', the servants at George Booth's establishment whose Christmas presents are described in detail, young Hatherley whose trust is being pillaged, Mrs Murberry who cannot understand her affairs, financial or otherwise. Neither Chislehurst nor the Voysey offices exist in isolation. They and their occupants are firmly set in Edwardian life.

Alice Maitland, for all her independence of mind and her willingness to commit herself to Edward as he faces imprisonment, has always led the life of a reasonably comfortable Edwardian lady.

> ALICE: I'm supposed to be off to Egypt on the twenty-eighth for three months. No. I'm not ill. But, as I've never yet had anything to do except to look after myself, the doctor thinks Egypt might be . . . most beneficial.

However, her self-awareness and her admiration for Edward's courage finally give her stature. Like Ann Leete before her, and Miss Yates after her, she is not 'careful of her life'.

The nearest approach to a Shavian 'New Woman' is Beatrice, who chose to marry Hugh Voysey for money and who will part from him as soon as she has earned enough by her writing to support herself, atypically Shavian marriage of convenience. It is she who realises that the House of Voysey needs regeneration, 'some fresh impulse to assert itself . . . I expect that is what a class needs to keep it socially alive.'

Mr Voysey has indeed provided one kind of 'fresh impulse', albeit warped, but Edward, like Ann Leete, must provide a purer one. By their actions, necessarily involving a loss of material comfort, they will revitalise a dying or poisoned or decadent stock.

The play abounds in naturalistic business as well as in naturalistically drawn characters. People eat and drink, smoke cigars, read periodicals, write letters and sew while conversing with each other, seemingly inconsequentially, but always revealing themselves and their beliefs and frequently illustrating a facet of the main argument. The constant flow of domestic activity provides the dramatic action in a play that is really a debate. The rooms are solid and three-dimensional, but at the same time they make a thematic statement. The Act I setting in Mr Voysey's office has the appearance of being polished and prosperous like its occupant. There are fresh roses, for after all Mr Voysey is a keen gardener and makes frequent reference to his celery, his strawberry plants and his apple trees. When Edward has taken over, the gleam has gone. There are no flowers. Not outward show, but mundane industry must now save the Voysey House. A change of setting that is explicable in naturalistic terms also brings the theme home to the audience visually. The portrait of the elder Voysey dominates the dining room at Chislehurst after his death, and he looks down on the discussion between Alice and Edward, reminding the audience of the cause of their perplexity.

Barker's production of his own play was one of the highlights of the Court season. It was ideally suited to the company, demanding close ensemble playing and detailed observation and presentation of characters. Barker was the perfect director for it with his ability to create the *milieu* and the lifestyle of a social class on stage.

'Waste'

Waste fits thematically as well as chronologically between

The Voysey Inheritance and *The Madras House*. The 'hero', Henry Trebell, begins this play in the same way as Edward Voysey ends the earlier work as 'a man without formulas'. He alleges that the world can do without dogma, and he personally has rejected rigid adherence to the doctrines of the church and of both the Liberal and the Tory politicians. The place and purpose of women in the social order, the main theme of *The Madras House*, is introduced in *Waste*. But the man of independent mind and the plight of women are treated more harshly and more pessimistically than in either of the other plays.

Waste, written in 1907, and intended for production at the Savoy in that year, was banned by the Lord Chamberlain. Barker took this very hard, and in a letter to Gilbert Murray (30 November 1907) complained that '*Waste* has wasted me.' The ban on the play was one of the incidents which inspired the petition of authors to the Prime Minister which led to the establishment of the Joint Committee oin the Censorship in 1909. The ostensible reason for the ban was the reference to Amy's abortion, but Barker, with some justification was cynical. In his evidence to the Select Committee, Barker stated '. . . he [Redford, the Lord Chamberlain's reader of plays] demanded that I should "eliminate entirely all reference to a criminal operation". I had myself produced at the Court Theatre a few months before under the Lord Chamberlain's licence a play the plot of which partly turned upon a criminal operation which was quite openly referred to on the stage.' He was referring to Elizabeth Robins' *Votes for Women!* produced at the Court in 1906. It was probably the unsympathetic representation of politicians, rather than the abortion issue, which caused the veto.

The Stage Society gave a private performance of *Waste* in November 1907, and the play, with the omissions required by the Censor, was given a reading for copyright purposes on Tuesday 28 January 1908, with Laurence Housman reading Trebell and Shaw's wife, Charlotte, reading Amy O'Connell. St John Hankin was George Farrant, John (called 'Joy') Galsworthy was Russell Blackborough and Lillah McCarthy read the part of the maid, Simson. Other participants included H.G. Wells (Gilbert Wedgecroft), Gilbert Murray (Lord Charles Cantelupe), William Archer (Justin O'Connell) and Shaw (The Earl of Horsham). The play was rewritten by Barker for a projected production in 1927, which did not take place until 1936. Although some substantial alterations in dialogue were made, in bringing the play 'up-to-date', the story and the characters remain the same in the two versions. It is the earlier version that is considered here, since it demonstrates more clearly the development of Barker's playwriting at this stage of his career.

As in most of Barker's dramatic work, the plot is less important than the issues that are raised in the course of the narrative. Henry Trebell, a distinguished and successful lawyer, is being courted by the Tory party in opposition, so that he can steer through Parliament a Bill to disestablish the Church. Trebell sees the vast sums that would result being turned over to education, which he believes is the only sound investment for the future. At a political houseparty, he meets Amy O'Connell, a pretty woman who is estranged from her husband in Ireland. He is sexually attracted to her, and the result of their one brief encounter is that she becomes pregnant. She is terrified of childbirth, and, although Trebell promises her every material support, she has a 'backstreet' abortion and dies. Although her husband, Justin, out of respect of Trebell, promises to remain silent at the inquest, the Tory Shadow Cabinet, ultimately for political rather than moral reasons, drops Trebell. He kills himself. The *Waste* of the title refers both to the waste of Amy and her unborn child, and to the waste of Trebell and of his visionary scheme of education.

Barker's treatment of the abortion issue is startlingly modern. Whereas Amy may be seen initially as a pretty, frivolous creature, who is quite out of place with the highly intellectual political and academic women in whose company she finds herself, preferring Chopin to Bach and bleating about her neuralgia, her defence of her position *vis à vis* childbirth is moving and powerful. She claims unequivocally that she has the right to choose whether or not to bear children. Had she stayed with her husband, done her wifely duty and borne his children, 'What would be left of me at all I should like to know?' The sentiment is echoed later by Frances Trebell, Henry's sister, whose intelligence and integrity are never in doubt. 'A woman must choose what her interpretation of life is to be . . . as a man must too in his way.' Later she reprimands her brother, 'You mustn't blame a woman for not wishing to bear children.' The 'woman's right to choose' is upheld.

But Barker makes it clear that the father has rights as well, and more significantly perhaps, instinctive emotions closely linked to the unborn child. As John Tanner asks in Shaw's *Man and Superman*, 'Is there a father's heart as well as a mother's?', Henry Trebell asserts that 'The man bears the child in his soul, as the woman carries the body.' His reaction to Amy's announcement of her pregnancy is one of wonderment, 'I am told that a man begins to feel important from this moment forward. Perhaps it's true.' Like Ann Leete and Marion Yates in *The Madras House*, Trebell places less emphasis on the relationship between the parents than he does on the child and is a tacit believer in the notion of the 'Life Force'. As Amy pleads for some acknowledgement from him that a form of romantic love existed between them at the moment of their child's conception, his response is cool, 'Only within the last five minutes have I taken the smallest interest in you.' He talks of their encounter in terms of procreation. 'Is it less of a purpose because we didn't know we had it?' He later condemns her for 'the misuse and waste of the only force there is in the world'. The bond, very quickly established between Amy's husband, Justin, and Trebell in the short scene between them in Act III, is based on Justin's sympathy with Trebell's 'sense of fatherhood'. He asserts Amy's worthlessness, and is bitterly aware of the wrong she has done him, not in having intercourse with Trebell, but in refusing to bear children, 'Is the curse of barrenness to be nothing to a man?'

As the two men celebrate life, Amy seems to them to deny it. She sees her pregnancy as reducing her to 'a savage', 'an animal', 'a sick beast in danger of my life, that's all . . . cancerous'. Trebell is appalled, 'Oh you unhappy woman, when life is like death to you'. Justin condemns her for her 'fear of the burden of her womanhood', as Trebell talks of 'The fear of life . . . do you think it was...which is the beginning of all evil?'

Intellectually, the argument is loaded in favour of the men. In their worlds of scholarship and visionary political reform, Amy is worthless for all but bearing their children. When she fails to do so, their scorn is unconcealed. Trebell recognises that Amy's philosophy is 'never to be reckless'. She is 'careful of her life', and so would appear to stand condemned in contrast to Ann Leete, Edward Voysey, Marion Yates and Philip Madras in Barker's personal scale of values. Yet there are extenuating circumstances. In the first place, her education has been hopelessly inadequate. She was taught 'the whole duty of woman by a parson-uncle who believed in his church', a clear link with the theme of education taking the place of religion after Disestablishment, and she asks, 'What education besides marriage does a woman get?' She appears at a considerable disadvantage in the company of the politically aware and highly literate ladies in Act I, who really rather despise her decorative frivolity. But the use which they are making of their educational advantages is also open to criticism. In addition, Trebell may be an idealistic reformer but his treatment of Amy is insensitive at best. His philosophical belief in 'Life' does not extend to understanding the weakness of its creatures, and his evident dislike of most women – his sister being an obvious exception – makes him see one half of the human race, not as individuals, but merely as bearers of the next generation. Amy needs more than the assurance that she will be well cared for during her pregnancy and that her child will be looked after. As Frances points out to her brother after Amy's death, it was in part his treatment of her that made her what she was, 'She became what you thought her', 'a pretty little fool'. She blames his contempt for men and women, 'Human nature turns against you . . . by instinct . . . in self-defence.' Trebell did not love her, and so Amy chooses to have the 'cancer' cut out, to have an abortion. The 'non-maternal' woman is, therefore, not wholly condemned, but seen as a victim of her circumstances, forced from an early age to play a role for which she is psychologically unsuited.

In reading the play, the argument that Amy's sin against life can warrant no forgiveness is dominant but in the playing of it she comes over as a much more sympathetic character. Hannah Gordon, in the BBC television production, using the 1927 script, played her as an intelligent woman using her only weapon, her physical attraction, to make an impact on a male-dominated world. Tragically, she is hoist by her own petard. If it is true that *Waste* was banned because of its treatment of the abortion issue, the Lord Chamberlain's reader could not have understood the play at all. *Waste* is not like Garnett's *The Breaking Point*, an overt plea for a relaxation of the abortion laws, and the whole question of the 'illegal operation' is secondary to the moral and philosphical issues. The amiable Dr Wedgecroft whose dramatic function is that of an enlightened and progressive *raisonneur*, is indecisive about whether or not he would have performed the operation or, had he known the facts, recommended to Amy a more reputable doctor. He condemns wholeheartedly, however, the charlatanism of the backstreet abortionist. But ultimately, the medical profession is to blame,'. . . that all comes of letting a trade work mysteriously under the thumb of a benighted oligarchy'. This indictment of the medical profession could equally well be applied to the politicians.

The theme of women's contribution to society is explored in *Waste*, although it is not as developed as in *The Madras House*. There is Amy, the woman who is mortally afraid of childbirth, Julia Farrant, a political hostess whose power lies in her influence over her husband and more significantly over Lord Horsham, the future Tory leader, Lucy Davenport, the fiancée of Trebell's secretary, Walter Kent, and Frances Trebell, Henry's sister. Each of these women is accomplished, astute and well-educated. There is also Lady Davenport, Julia's mother, who sees herself as being apart from the active world of politics, yet is still perfectly capable of injecting apposite remarks into the conversation.

The play opens with Julia playing through the whole of a Chopin prelude, although most of the company prefers Bach. Lucy has a book by a German philosopher on her lap. Frances has been a successful and highly respected schoolmistress. It is natural that such women, although placed as befits their sex in a drawing-room after dinner, should talk of politics and of education. They recognise the frustration of having to assert themselves through men. Julia, when told that her future lies in helping Cyril Horsham to govern the country may acknowledge the suggestion with a coy laugh, but Frances Trebell is quite specific, 'Till I was forty I never realised the fact that most women must express themselves through men.' Julia recognises a worthy successor in Lucy Davenport, 'She will have him [Walter Kent] in the Cabinet by the time he's fifty.' Lady Davenport may quote Disraeli's diction that 'Clever women are as dangerous to the State as dynamite' but Frances is quick to cap it, 'Well, Lady Davenport, if men will leave our intellects lying loose about . . .'. The other women are little better than Amy, for they continue to 'work through men', just as Amy must define herself by attempting to attract them.

It is because of this influence on men, that Henry Trebell hates women. When Wedgecroft commends women's tradition of service', Trebell's reply is sour, 'Slavery . . . not quite the same thing. And the paradox of slavery is that they're your only tyrants. One has to be optimistic not to advocate the harem.' Trebell's views on the role of women correspond almost to the letter with those of Constantine in *The Madras House*. Just as the latter sees women's involvement in public life as enervating, so Trebell despises the 'compromise, tenderness, pity, lack of purpose' into which women trap those who fall under their influence. Both men father a child as the result of a casual encounter, both are anxious to provide for it, at least materially, and in both cases, this is denied to them by the actions of the women involved.

In this portrayal of the character of Henry Trebell, a man who is confident enough in his own ethical and political values to eschew adherence to any orthodox morality or political system, Barker shows the weaknesses of a position advocated in an earlier work. Edward Voysey grows in stature as he sheds received and conventional views on morality and religion. Much is made in the opening scene of *Waste* of Trebell's unwillingness to see himself as a member of any party. He is, in the words of Wedgecroft, 'grown-up enough to do without dogma', 'a man without formulas', as he describes himself to Cantelupe. But Wedgecroft warns that 'perfect balance is most easily lost' and Frances recognises the weakness in such independence, 'I think it's a mistake to stand outside a system. There's an inhumanity in that amount of detachment.' Trebell, despite his humanitarian passion for educational reform, appreciates humanity in the abstract, not in the particular. His zeal for his reforms is the result partly of his intellectual appreciation of the neatness of his scheme and partly of the fascination he finds in the means of accomplishing it. His desire for the child derives from an ideal of fatherhood, rather than from the physical need for a real baby. He displays little interest in 'Cousin Mary's new baby' despite the fact that he has previously asserted that only 'Birth, Death and the Desire for children can produce real emotion.' His shortlived sexual attraction to Amy, he dismisses as 'the silliest vice'.

Until the last act, he is passionate only in his deep-seated belief in the value of education, which is, as he admits, his 'religion'. It is partly the waste of this passion, that gives the play its title, and the resulting tragedy is almost classical in form. Trebell's flaw, his lack of compassion and sympathy for indivduals, causes the waste of his educational vision, which is, like his child, aborted. Trebell, himself, draws the parallel, 'When [a man] loses a seat in the Cabinet he turns inward for comfort . . . and if he only finds there a spirit which should have been born, but is dead . . . what's to be done then?'

Ironically, it is not the scandal involving Amy and her child that causes the Tory party to exclude Trebell from the future Cabinet, but self-interested party politics. At the beginning of the discussion Cantelupe, the high-principled churchman, finds it morally impossible to serve with Trebell, but, ultimately, for the sake of the benefits to the nation that would result from increased educational opportunity, he is prepared to disregard his moral scruples. Trebell is rejected as the result of the arguments of Blackborough, who clearly puts party politics before national need. Trebell's inclusion he believes would split the Tory party and lose the election. The 'Amy' affair only provides the excuse to dismiss him. Cantelupe's question at the end of the discussion, 'From what motives have we thrown Trebell over?' is as illuminating as Blackborough's reply, 'Never mind the motives if the move is the right one.' It is to Bach (not to Chopin) that Cantelupe turns in his doubt and regret, 'all that ability turned to destructiveness . . . what a pity!' The Act ends, however, with Cantelupe and the future Prime Minister discussing their aunt's idiosyncratic desire to sell a painting by Holbein. One might well agree with some of Barker's contemporaries that it was the political satire of *Waste* rather than the mention of an illegal operation that caused the play to be banned.

The Madras House

The Madras House was first performed at the Duke of York's Theatre in London as part of Charles Frohman's Repertory Season in March 1909. It has been revived twice, in November 1925 at the Ambassadors Theatre, and more recently, by the National Theatre in June 1977.

The play cannot fail to strike a modern audience or reader as one of the most searching investigations of the place of women in society ever written. Although it was first performed over seventy years ago at a time when feminist issues had rather a different focus, namely the struggle for the vote, its examination of the problems of the woman's role and of sexual politics remains perceptive. The 1890s and early 1900s saw a spate of plays that had women as subjects, the most celebrated being Pinero's *The Second Mrs Tanqueray* and Jones's *Mrs Dane's Defence*. The women in such works were the protagonists, a device borrowed from Ibsen although much diluted by the English dramatists. Although the heroine enjoys the title role, the plays make statements not so much about the women themselves, but about a male-dominated society's attitudes to them. The women are used to define the men.

Barker reverses this process. His protagonist, Philip Madras (and protagonist is rather too active a word for Philip's dramatic function in the play) finds his opinions and attitudes are shaped by the women he encounters. Even in the opening stage direction the descriptions of each of the six Huxtable daughters who appear only in Act I and have only a few lines each, are longer and more detailed than that of Philip, the hero, or more accurately, the 'linkman' of the play. The thumbnail sketches of the Huxtable girls demonstrate Barker's skill as a director, in that each detail he gives is of great value to the actress in building her character: 'artistic' Julia, who conceals her inadequate watercolours with tears of frustration; 'practical' Laura who wins a silent victory in putting the Chinese umbrella rather than ferns in the empty summer fireplace, because the former gathers less dust. Such points help the actress to create the flesh to clothe the few lines she is given,

and provide the three-dimensional quality that characte-
rises Barker's dramas. It is as if Stanislavsky had written
stage directions for Chekhov's plays, and shows Barker's
difference from Shaw, whose character descriptions,
however witty, often tell us more about the author and his
philosophy than about the character. William Gaskill, who
directed *The Madras House* for the National Theatre,
instructed his actors to observe the stage directions closely
in their playing.

Philip Madras is confronted in each of the four acts by
women of different social backgrounds and with different
problems. Only Jessica, his wife, and Amelia, his mother,
make two appearances, and the first one in each case is
brief. Barker is as prodigal with characters as he was in the
fourth act of *Ann Leete*, but in the later play they are more
tightly integrated to his theme, stated in the opening
seconds of the play by Philip, 'Well, my dear Tommy, what
are the two most important things in a man's character? His
attitude towards money and his attitude towards women.'
There is virtually no narrative plot. We are told at the
outset that Philip is going to give up his interest in the
Madras House, a high-class fashion house and that he
intends to stand for the County Council, with an idea of
effecting radical reforms in social conditions. He does. The
business transactions take a few lines, and although Philip
discusses the reasons for his change of direction, the
audience does not see him agonising over the decision. His
mind is made up long before the play opens.

The two aspects of the theme, 'attitudes to money' and
'attitudes to women' are linked in that we are guided to the
conclusion, by being shown a wide range of examples, that
the unsatisfactory position of women in society is the result
of deeper social evils, class distinctions and physical
deprivation, and the only way that women's plight on

whatever level can be improved is by a radical reform of society itself.

The play opens and closes in a domestic setting. The first act takes place in the drawing room of the Huxtables, a cosy prison for the eight women who inhabit it. The adjoining conservatory, where an agapanthus blooms and a frog dies, which events provide some little excitement for the six unmarried daughters of the household, reflects in minia-ture the Crystal Palace that can be viewed from its windows. Much is made of the view of this edifice, part fairy-tale castle and part symbol of the 'self help' principle, a monument to 'the working bees of the world's hive', to which number Huxtable *père* belongs. Act IV is set in Jessica's grey and pink drawing room, elegant in its furnishings as befits its mistress. Jessica's drawing-room is for her a refuge from the reality of the social deprivation that exists outside, but as Philip makes clear to her, she will only find the solution to her own problems as a woman by leaving this shrine to civilisation, good taste and culture, and by coming with him to face the ugliness and dirt of the slums.

PHILIP: (*He surveys the charming room that is his home*). Persian carpet on the floor. Last Supper by Ghirlanda-jo over the mantelpiece. The sofa you're sitting on was made in a forgotten France. This is a museum.

Domestic settings were commonly used in the 'drawing room drama', especially in plays about women, for the obvious reason that it was in the home that most women spent most of their time. Barker endows each of his two rooms with a distinct character, that not only reflects its inhabitants but demonstrates in terms of stage design the obstacles to individual freedom which they must face.

Jessica's drawing room is less cluttered than the Huxtables', her maid is less 'becapped and aproned', but despite outward expansiveness Phillimore Gardens gives no more true liberty than Denmark Hill.

Acts II and III are set in the Madras Fashion House, the first in an anteroom to Philip's office, the second in the Moorish rotunda designed by Philip's father, Constantine Madras. The audience is, a rare thing in the drama of the period, confronted by women at work. In Act II, there is Miss Chancellor, the housekeeper, in charge of the young ladies who live in the premises and Miss Yates, one of the shop assistants. In Act III, there is the battery of exotic mannequins. The use of the waiting room is obviously convenient as a dramatic location that can bring people together, but it is also neutral ground for the contesting parties, and its drabness compared to the Eastern pastiche of the public room in Act III shows the work-a-day world behind the veneer presented to the public, just as Miss Yates changes from her natural manner to her 'customer manner' when Jessica enters. The Moorish rotunda, an early expression of Constantine's fascination with the East, is a fitting setting for the seraglio of mannequins and their eunuch, Windlesham. It is rich, lavish, decorative and false, 'about as Moorish as Baker Street Station'.

In the journey from the Huxtable home in Primrose Hill on Sunday morning to his place of work on Monday and back to his, or rather Jessica's, elegant drawing room in Phillimore Gardens that evening, Philip Madras is confronted by fourteen women and becomes involved in a prolonged discussion with his father and Eugene State, the American buyer of the fashion house, on 'the place of women in society'. His views are not altered by the day's experience, but rather confirmed. He is described at the outset as 'kind in manner but rather cold, capable of that

least English of dispositions – intellectual passion'. Deirdre
Clancy, the designer of the National Theatre production,
copied his first act costume from a photograph of Barker,
but, although it may be reasonable to assume some features
of a self-portrait, Philip is not necessarily always a spokesman for the author. He is for most of the play, until the last
scene with Jessica, a detached and benevolent observer
who guides the audience gently to the desired point of view.

The six unmarried daughters of the Huxtable household
display their barren life in their repetitious conversation (a
technique previously used by Barker to dramatise the
sterility of the Sarah/Lord Arthur relationship in *The
Marrying of Ann Leete*). The repetition of the naturalistic
introductions of the girls to Major Thomas, Philip's
companion, the chorus of 'How do you do's, followed by
the inevitable 'Will you stay to dinner?' is comic, and at the
same time underlines the similarity of the women's plight,
even if Barker takes care to differentiate their characters.
These subtleties evade Mr Huxtable who tends to confuse
one with another. Emma 'who would have been a success in
an office and worth perhaps thirty shillings a week',
becomes a spokesman for her sisters but not in order to
bemoan their lot.

PHILIP: Are you all happy now, then?
EMMA: Oh, deep down, I think we are. It would be so
    ungrateful not to be. When one has a good home
    and . . .

And what, one wonders? Despite the shared bedrooms and
the rather tight-fisted attitude of their father, the girls have
'lots to do about the house and there's calling and classes
and things'. Philip's suggestion that they all leave fills
Emma with horror:

EMMA (*wide-eyed*): Go away!

PHILIP (*comprehensively*): Out of it.

EMMA (*wider-eyed*): Where to?

PHILIP (*with a sigh – for her*): Ah, that's just it.

EMMA: How could one! And it would upset them dreadfully. Father and mother don't know that one feels like this at times . . . they'd be very grieved.

And so, the Huxtable girls (for they are still girls, although the youngest is twenty-six) will stay in their comfortable nest, making occasionally flurries for freedom, like Jane's rebellion when her suitor was rejected by her parents, or indulging in adolescent fantasies, like the thirty-four year old Julia swooning over Lewis Waller's collar and crying when her mother removed it. They will continue to be told when to keep their hats on, asked where they are going when they leave the room and mildly reprimanded for taking the long way home from church – the lot of the unemployed, unmarried women of the middle class at the turn of the century.

Philip compares the situation at Denmark Hill to the living-in system for the employees at Mr Huxtable's shop, thus linking the plight of the six spinsters with their dominant mother and that of the workers in Act II and the formidable Miss Chancellor. Although the Huxtable girls might well have been happier had they been able to undertake some form of paid employment, Barker is at pains to show in Act II that the women who have a reasonable degree of financial independence, in that they are wage-earners, are not without problems. Marion Yates, a highly-respected shop assistant, has become pregnant. She refuses to reveal the name of the child's father, but when Miss Chancellor, the housekeeper, sees her being kissed, albeit in a fairly fraternal manner, by

Brigstock, the 'Third Man in Hosiery', she jumps to the wrong conclusion and accuses him. The latter is married, but because of the living-in system is parted from his wife, who is outraged by the housekeeper's nasty words. The four sit in the dingy waiting room ready to confront Philip.

The living-in system to which Philip likened the lives of the Huxtable daughters in Act I is represented as the reason for the unmarried state of Miss Yates and the childless one of Mrs Brigstock. The lot of the respectable middle-class girls condemned to leisure is compared to that of the working-class women, and the living-in system can be seen as a metaphor for the constricting role that society forces on its female members. It is true that Miss Chancellor and Miss Yates are not dependent on a man's whim for their pin money, but the former is quick to point out that financial independence does not mean spiritual liberation, 'Because a woman is independent and earning her living she's not to think she can go on as she pleases.' But Miss Chancellor, despite her puritanical attitude to Miss Yates's pregnancy, does put forward, albeit partly as a justification for her own life, the view that marriage is not the only valid alternative for a woman:

> Is there nothing for a woman to do in the world but to run after men . . . or pretend to run away from them? I am fifty-eight . . . and I have passed, thank God, a busy and a happy and I hope a useful life . . . and I have never thought any more or less of men than I have of any other human beings . . . or any differently. I look upon spinsterhood as an honourable state, as my Bible teaches me to.

Despite the sanctimonious tone of her remarks, at least Miss Chancellor has progressed further on the path to liberation than Julia Huxtable with her adolescent 'pash' on Lewis Waller. Her remark that she has never viewed men and women differently links her with Philip who is trying, and often succeeding, to do likewise. As he says, he tries to put himself in Miss Yates's place, and later in a conversation with Major Thomas, he claims to have this notion as the basis for his treatment of women:

> THOMAS: You can't behave towards women as if they were men.
> PHILIP: Why not?
> THOMAS: You try it!
> PHILIP: I always do.

He talks to Miss Yates as 'man to man' and he treats his wife 'as a man would treat another man'. Jessica recognises that her husband's attitude is an advance on the flirtatious levity and facile admiration of Major Thomas.

> JESSICA: I'm well off married to you, I know. You do make me forget I'm a female occasionally.

But there is shown to be a real difference between the sexes especially in a society that demands comfortable stereotypes, in which as Philip puts it, the male and the female have not yet grown into men and women.

Miss Yates is seen as the embodiment of the 'Life Force'. She 'glows in that room like a live coal. She has genius – she has life.' Her determination not to reveal the name of her child's father and to deny him any rights in its upbringing and her courage in facing the prejudiced world alone with the baby are admirable qualities to Philip and, therefore, to the audience. Miss Yates is applauded, as Ann Leete was, for refusing to be 'careful of her life'. In *Waste*, Amy

O'Connell is criticised for her lack of courage. For all three the decision to assert an independent identity is closely linked to birth, and the unborn child seems to be more important than the man who fathered it. But Barker does not have any sentimental romantic view of motherhood. It is made clear that Miss Yates will have to struggle materially and psychologically to preserve her independence. Like Ann Leete's, her future is promising in its brave new beginning but it is not an easy walk into the sunset of happy-ever-after. The cant of the Maternal is satirised by Barker in Act III, when State talks, in capital letters of 'the noblest Instinct of all . . . the Instinct to Perpetuate our Race'.

At the end of Act II, the audience sees Philip with his wife, Jessica, 'the result – not of thirty-five years – but of three or four generations of cumulative refinement'. William Gaskill saw her as a reflection of Barker's wife, Lillah McCarthy, and held that this part was the most difficult to cast in the whole play. She appears to have all the physical and social advantages that the other women lack. The gulf between Jessica and 'the rest' is dramatised at once by the change in Miss Yates's manner on the entrance of the former. The lack of a feeling of sisterhood or consciousness of a common cause among women has already been intimated in Miss Yates's remarks about her experiences as a shop assistant in the fashionable Bond Street branch of the Madras House. 'Those ladies that you get there . . . well, it does just break your nerve. What with following them about and the things they say you've got to hear, and the things they'll say . . . about you, half the time . . . that you've got not to hear'. The women, including Jessica, who calls Miss Yates 'an ugly little woman' are more conscious of their class differences than of the similarities of their plight. Jessica cuts herself off by her aesthetic and cultural pursuits. It is typical of her that she comments adversely on Miss Yates's physical appearance, failing to recognise as Philip does, the woman's attractiveness. She interrupts the work of the office to take Philip, or failing him, Major Thomas off to an art gallery. While it is easy to criticise Jessica's attitudes, they are partly the result of Philip's treatment of her. He is so preoccupied with trying to put his own 'house' in order that until Act IV he fails to appreciate her difficulties. He deals much more sympathetically and seriously with Miss Yates. But he recognises that the tension that lurks just below the surface in the scene with his wife is the result of the gender roles that each is forced to play by social conditions and conditioning.

> PHILIP: We've so organised the world's work as to make companionship between men and women a very artificial thing.

The brief scene between Jessica and Philip is only a foretaste for the long discussion between them in Act IV, but its place in the dramatic structure is interesting in inviting a comparison between Miss Yates and Jessica, and in demonstrating not just Philip's predisposition for theory over practice in his relationships with women, but also the response of Major Thomas, 'the mean sensual man', to a beautiful woman, namely to flirt with her, and then to run away from her attractiveness.

In Act III, in the sumptuous Moorish pavilion the mannequins parade in the latest Paris fashions before the directors of the Madras House and the prospective American buyer, Eugene State. Here the feminist point is clear. Clothes and women alike are viewed as objects, and there is only a little margin to be drawn between the elegant Jessica, exhibiting her person to attract Philip or Major

Thomas, and the models parading before the ogling men. Setting out to attract men for the purpose of some form of personal gain is seen to be the common cause of the courtesan, the mannequin and the fashionable lady:

> PHILIP (*heartlessly*): La belle Helene, Mr State, is a well-known Parisian cocotte . . . who sets many of the fashions which our wives and daughters afterwards assume.
>
> MR HUXTABLE (*scandalised*): Don't say that, Phil; it's not nice.
>
> PHILIP: Why?
>
> MR HUXTABLE: I'm sure no ladies are aware of it.
>
> PHILIP: But what can be more natural and right than for the professional charmer to set the pace for the amateur?
>
> MR STATE (*solemnly*): Do you infer, Mr Madras, a difference in degree, but not in kind?
>
> PHILIP (*courteously echoing his tone*): I do.

The dresses emphasise not only the purely decorative qualities of the women, but also the artificial distance between the sexes. The models cannot even sit down in the dresses, and they offer the men the sexual titillation of the coquette or the creature of male fantasy. Philip calls one dress 'a conspiracy in three colours on the part of half a dozen sewing women to persuade you the creature they have clothed can neither walk, digest her food, nor bear children.' The exquisite untouchable model can never be regarded as an equal of man, not even as a fellow human being. Windlesham handles the mannequins only as objects, adjusting their clothes as if they were statues, and State admits that it is easy to forget their existence. He continues, 'We gave some time and money to elaborating a mechanical moving figure to take the place of . . . a real automaton, in fact. But sometimes it stuck and sometimes it ran away . . .'. One feels that the robots may have shown more initiative than the mannequins who are always referred to by number and who are moved mechanically by Windlesham's remote control.

Eugene State seeks to elevate his commercial enterprises by endowing them with a philosophical ideal. His justification for extending his activities into the arena of women's fashion is his belief in 'The Great Modern Woman's Movement'. He has attended meetings on the 'Woman Question' all over England and has come to the conclusion that 'The Woman's Movement is Woman expressing herself . . . What are a woman's chief means . . . how often her only means of expressing herself? Any way . . . what is the first thing that she spends her money on? Clothes, gentlemen, Clothes.' He sees his contribution to the liberation of women as giving to middle-class woman the opportunity of revealing her personality through dress. 'I want to see that Poor Provincial Lady burst through the laurel bushes and dash down the road . . . Clad in the Colours of the Rainbow.' At this point Major Thomas offers the model who has been standing around for some time, a chair. Windlesham intervenes, 'Thank you . . . but she can't. Not in that corset.' Fashionable dress is physically restricting, and the likelihood of its being spiritually liberating is remote. But State's ideals have an economic aspect as well. He is well aware that 'the Middle Class Women of England' are 'one of the Greatest Money Spending Machines the world has ever seen.' He looks forward to the economic independence of women in the confidence that even more cash will find its way into his registers. The States of the world will continue, under the guise of liberating women, to exploit them for financial gain.

Constantine Madras, Philip's father, the creator of the Moorish pavilion and the head of the Madras House, presents a much more seductive argument. William Gaskill thought that one of the major problems of directing the piece was to avoid Constantine becoming the dominant character and his point of view from becoming the 'message' of the play. Constantine is opposed to all Western ideas or fantasies about women, and finds the mannequins, the pretentious ideas of State and the middle-class ethics of the Huxtables distasteful, and indeed immoral. 'Europe in its attitude towards women is mad.' Constantine preaches, in direct opposition to his son, that men and women are so fundamentally different that the whole notion of equality is absurd. Women, more than one woman it should be made clear, since Constantine is a convert to Mohammedanism, should be waiting at home 'unharassed by notions of business or, politics . . . ready to refresh one's spirit by attuning it to the gentler, sweeter side of life.' His argument is that the male function and the female function are different, and that confusion leads to chaos. The involvement of women in politics has been 'softening, sentimental, enervating'. Nationalism, Justice and Religion have been diminished through female influence into anger, kindness and pretty hymn tunes. Where Constantine scores is that he is quick to point out the financial exploitation of women by State and even by Huxtable. Talking of the employees, he says, 'How much do they rejoice in their freedom to earn their living by ruining their health and stifling their instincts?' Huxtable is virtually accused of being a pimp because he puts his shop assistants like Miss Yates 'on exhibition for ten hours a day . . . their good looks, their good manners, their womanhood . . . For such treatment of potential motherhood, my Prophet condemns a man to Hell.' The dehumanising of the mannequins disgusts him equally. Constantine's solution, the return to polygamy, can hardly be accepted. He is after all the father of Miss Yates's child – a fact that William Gaskill thought was a flaw in the play, but which serves to discredit Constantine's morals and his philosophy – and secondly, Jessica, so politely, rejects his courtesies in Act IV. His projected visit to Voysey – one assumes that he is referring to Voysey *père* – is perhaps meant to indicate to those with knowledge of the earlier play that his financial legacies both to Miss Yates and to Mildred, Philip's daughter, may not materialise.

The fourth and final act is mostly taken up with a discussion between Philip and his wife. The object of at least part of their dispute – Jessica and Philip would not quarrel – is their daughter, Mildred, who will have to leave her expensive school, when Philip relinquishes his commercial interests and becomes a member of the County Council. The salvation of the Madras House, like the House of Leete, lies with a girl. According to Philip, the only useful thing that Mildred is learning is gardening. For the rest, she is only being instructed in the arts of cultured upper middle-class civilisation of which her mother is an accomplished exponent. Jessica questions the alternative, 'But what is it we're to cultivate in poor Mildred's soul?' Philip replies uncompromisingly, 'a sense of ugliness.' Philip wants his daughter to eschew the civilisation and culture, 'the very latest of class distinctions', that both he and Jessica love. He wants for her instead the ability to feel with the prostitute and the murderer, to improve, not to despise, the alternative civilisation of Whitechapel Road. Finally, Philip and Jessica meet 'halfway'. The implication is that Jessica will, despite the difficulties of which she is fully aware, cease to be a 'lady', and follow her husband's advice to 'Come out and be common women among us common men.' The end of the discussion is the end of the play, unfinished 'for there is really no end to the subject'. But there is optimism. Jessica is capable of throwing off the attitudes which are the products of her education, 'to be charming and to like dainty clothes'. Mildred's new education will fit her better for a new world, with 'a culture that shan't be just a veneer on savagery'. Although the last scene has been thought to be dramatically redundant, it is thematically necessary. Jessica, the finest flower of élitism, must be seen to be at least partially convinced of the need for change. Her consciousness as a woman and as a socially responsible individual must be raised to the point where she understands the implications of the play's theme, that the only way in which a woman can achieve status in society is by reform of society as a whole.

2
John Galsworthy

John Galsworthy was born on 14 August 1867, the son of a wealthy solicitor. Educated at Harrow and at New College, Oxford, he began, unenthusiastically and unsuccessfully, to practise Law. In 1895, encouraged by his cousin's wife, Ada Galsworthy, whom he was later to marry, and by his sister, Lilian, he decided to become a writer. At first, he was no more successful as an author than he had been as a barrister. His collection of short stories, *From the Four Winds* and *Villa Rubein*, published under the pseudonym, John Sinjohn, went largely unnoticed, but Galsworthy believed that good writers were made, not born. He was greatly helped by the advice and friendship of Joseph Conrad, whom he had first met during a voyage to Capetown in 1892, and most especially by Edward Garnett, then a reader for the publishing house of Duckworth. Garnett and his wife, Constance, whose translations of the works of Turgenev were to influence Galsworthy's writing, became friends and constructive critics. The last volume which Galsworthy published under his pseudonym, *A Man of Devon* (1901), a collection of four long 'short' stories, introduced to the reading public the family of the Forsytes, and established Galsworthy firmly among the ranks of the 'promising'. Finally, after his long and painful apprenticeship, he achieved literary success in 1906 with the publication of *A Man of Property*, dedicated to Edward Garnett.

In the same year, Garnett, a staunch supporter of the Stage Society and the Court, suggested that Galsworthy turn his hand to writing for the theatre. Galsworthy responded with *The Silver Box*, the success of which was to establish him at once as one of the leaders of the 'new drama' movement. It was remarkable that Galsworthy achieved theatrical acclaim so quickly. It had after all taken him over ten years to establish his reputation as a novelist, and, on his own admission, he was 'in no sense a student of drama, nor a great playgoer',[1] although he had begun to write a play entitled *The Civilised* in 1901. He was reluctant to take up Garnett's suggestion, and only did so because he disliked the artificial nature of English drama and because he was determined to present real life on the stage.

The Silver Box, first produced at the Court in 1906, was followed by *Joy*, presented at the Savoy in 1907, *Strife* at the Duke of York's in 1909, and *Justice*, which opened Frohman's Repertory season at the Duke of York's in 1910. All four plays were directed by Granville Barker. They were very popular with the provincial Repertory Theatres, Manchester in particular.

With typical assiduity, Galsworthy involved himself in the production process. He was fully involved in discussions about casting, he attended rehearsals and corresponded with Barker about characterisation. Both men shared a faith in the primacy of the text in the theatrical process, and Barker, with his flair for detailed naturalistic and atmospheric production, was an excellent interpreter of Galsworthy's plays. The acting style that evolved at the Court was equally suited to give flesh and blood to his characters. Despite Galsworthy's good fortune in his theatrical associates which he fully acknowledged, and

1. Harley Granville Barker

2. John Galsworthy

3. John Masefield

4. *The Marrying of Ann Leete* Royal Shakespeare Company 1975. Oliver Cotton as Abud, Mia Farrow as Ann Leete

5. Mia Farrow as Ann Leete

6. *The Voysey Inheritance* Kingsway Theatre 1912.

7. *Waste,* Royal Shakespeare Company, 1985 Judi Dench as Amy and Maria Aitken as Frances Trebell

8. Judi Dench as Amy, David Massey as Trebell

9. *The Madras House* National Theatre 1976 Ronald Pickup as Philip, Helen Ryan as Jessica

10. Paul Schofield as Constantine and Mannequin

11. *Strife* The National Theatre 1978 Michael Bryant as Roberts, Andrew Cruikshank as Anthony

12. Brian Kent as Frost, Andrew Cruikshank as Anthony

despite the critical success of his plays, he preferred the novelistic to the dramatic form. The agony he suffered on first nights was legendary – his non-appearance before the rapturous audience of *Justice* caused considerable embarrassment to Barker and to the management – and he maintained that, no matter how successful a play had been, he always experienced personal dissatisfaction, 'a sense that one has not succeeded in conveying to more than a handful the sense and heart of the matter.'[2]

Galsworthy also professed that he found the dramatic mode restrictive, experiencing 'a limitation set to creative freedom by the form and conditions of the drama . . . I cannot quite shake off a sense of cramp in writing for the theatre.'[3] Despite these sentiments, he managed to adapt remarkably quickly to the constraints of playwriting and used to great effect techniques that he had learned during his ten years' apprenticeship as a novelist. He continued to write for the stage, even after the first reforming ardour of the 'new drama' movement had faded with the outbreak of the First World War. His most famous later plays were *The Skin Game* (1919), *Loyalties* (1921), *Escape* (1926) and *Exiled* (1929).

The Silver Box

Galsworthy began work on *The Silver Box* in January 1906 and completed the first draft within six weeks. Garnett suggested a few emendations, and the revised script was submitted to Barker in April. He and Shaw read the piece over a weekend and accepted it at once for production at the Court in the Autumn. There was to be a trial run of eight matinées, and if the play proved successful, it would be transferred to an evening bill for a short run. The matinée performances took place from 25 September to 19

October 1906, and the revival ran for three weeks in April 1907.

The plot is straightforward. Jack Barthwick, a wealthy young man, returns home late one evening, very drunk. He is assisted in entering his house by James Jones, an unemployed workman, who is equally 'under the influence'. Jack offers Jones whisky and cigarettes, and, before passing out on the sofa, tells him to 'take anything he wants'. Jones, further inebriated by Jack's hospitality, 'takes' the silver cigarette box and a lady's purse, which we learn from Jack's drunken maunderings, he has 'taken' from his lady companion of the evening, to 'score off her'.

The following morning it is discovered that the cigarette box is missing and Jones's wife, charwoman to the Barthwicks, is suspected of theft. The 'lady' whose purse had been stolen returns to claim it, and is paid off by Jack's father, a Liberal Member of Parliament, who is anxious to avoid any scandal. The Joneses' room is searched, the cigarette box is discovered, and Mrs Jones is charged. In an attempt to clear his wife and admit his own guilt, Jones assaults a police officer and is also taken into custody. Mr Barthwick realises that his son's crime will be revealed in the course of the Joneses' trial, and sets his lawyer to work to safeguard his reputation. In the final act, the Police Court scene, the Magistrate delivers a mild reprimand to Jack for his over-indulgence, and commits Jones to a month's hard labour.

The piece fitted very well into one category of dramas produced at the Court, plays described by Desmond MacCarthy as presenting 'a critical and dissenting attitude towards contemporary codes of morality'. The 'main idea' of the play, as Galsworthy described it, is 'that "one law for the rich, another for the poor" is true, but not because society wills it so, rather, in spite of society's good intentions, through the mechanical wide-branching power of money.'[4] This theme is worked through meticulously within the play. The elder Barthwick can pay to protect his reputation and his son's. Mrs Jones, through no fault of her own, loses her good name and her prospects of employment. Jack takes the 'lady's' bag', 'to score off her'. Jones takes the cigarette box, 'out of spite'. Jack had presumably been disappointed in his sexual advances. Jones's act can be seen as an act of revenge, however misguided, on a society that gave luxury to some yet failed to provide an opportunity to earn a living to others. The Magistrate smiles at Jack's admission that he had had too much champagne and deals indulgently with his total loss of recall of the incident. Jones's drunkenness is viewed much more censoriously.

It is in the Police Court scene that the parallels are most heavily underlined. The Magistrate, in talking to Jones repeats phrases that Mr Barthwick had previously used to Jack. Barthwick says to Jack in Act I, scene ii, 'You're one of those who are a nuisance to society.' The Magistrate calls Jones, 'A nuisance to the community.' Both Mr Barthwick and the Magistrate make the point that drunkenness is no excuse for criminal action. Each of these verbal echoes is underlined by Jack's drawing his father's, and incidentally the audience's, attention to them. And, lest the point has not been sufficiently hammered home, Jones reiterates it in his final speech:

> JONES: Call this justice? What about 'im? 'E got drunk. 'E took the purse – 'e took the purse but (*in a muffled shout*) it's 'is money got 'im off – *Justice!*

Despite the strong enunciation of the theme, Galsworthy was to deny throughout his life that he had written a propagandist play, and as far as *The Silver Box* is concerned, Galsworthy was right in insisting that it was not a play that preached political or social reform. The only 'solution' that is offered is that the fortunate members of society, like the Barthwicks, should, in the first place, have imagination enough to enable them to have sympathy for their less prosperous fellow men and, secondly, should have the courage to act according to their liberal principles. The problem, and in some ways *The Silver Box* is a 'problem' play, is a problem for the middle classes. It is this group that is being asked to reexamine its prejudices and its principles. It is to this group that the play is addressed, the group to which Galsworthy himself, and the majority of the Court audience, belonged. There is no suggestion that the Joneses could possibly take any positive action to improve their situation. Jones could 'opt out' by going to Canada, leaving his wife and children, but that idea is put forward very speculatively, and is not in any case altering the economic plight of the unemployed in Britain. The sympathetic working-class characters are distinguished by their passivity. The good sober workman, Livens, acquiesces humbly to the removal of his daughter to a children's home. There is, as he sees it, no alternative. 'The keynote of *Mrs Jones* is *passivity*', wrote Galsworthy to Granville Barker, 'and she must not be played pathetically, only *be* pathetic from force of circumstances.'[5] Even the Unknown Lady, 'must contrive to be pathetic, without seeming to try'. The passivity of the poor is partly commended, or at least viewed sympathetically, not criticised as in Shaw's work. It is Jones, the drunkard, the reprobate husband, who rebels. 'The keynote of Jones is smouldering revolt.' He attempts to state the working-class case in the Police Court scene, but one cannot help feeling that, just as he is silenced in the play by the formal legal procedure which is alien to him and which favours the middle class, Galsworthy, in addition, loads the dice against him by making him a bad husband with tendencies towards alcoholism. In a similar way, John Walker mitigated the social criticism of Rushton in *The Factory Lad*, by making him unbalanced as a result of the massacre of his family. There is no call to revolution, and the plea to those favoured by society for humanity and tolerance does not imply any advocacy of fundamental changes in the social order.

What Galsworthy did claim for the play was that it represented a complete break from contemporary dramatic form, and he took great pride in this. Yet although the playwright was attempting to avoid the artificialities of contemporary stage conventions, the play in its ethos is similar to nineteenth-century melodrama. In a letter to John Palmer in 1915, he wrote, '[My plays] are all founded in the emotions of love, pity, hatred and the "ideas" for them would hardly fill a teacup, unless by "ideas" are meant the main lines of feeling that hold all work together.'[6] In other words, he was knowingly using one of the principal melodramatic techniques, gaining effects by heightened emotional, rather than by intellectual, appeal. The Joneses' child crying for its mother outside the Barthwicks' house is reminiscent of the heart-rending song, 'Father, dear Father, come home' of Temperance melodrama, and the emotional *frisson* was exactly the effect for which he was striving. 'I keep the child's crying, because a physical thrill to the audience at this point is worth any added Barthwick psychology. You know my theory (founded on personal experience) that the physical emotional thrill is all that really counts in a play.'[7] *The Silver Box* has much in common with the ethics of Temperance melodrama. Jones is cruel to his wife because he drinks. Jack gets into trouble because he gets drunk. Livens' family is destroyed because his wife drank and deserted him and his children. It is the Mrs Jones's crying child and the story of the Livens' children weeping outside a public house – they are pathetically silent in the Police Court – that demonstrate in an emotional, or even in a sentimental, way the weakness of their parents. There is no Temperance spokesman to reform with his rhetoric, and some account is taken of the extenuating circumstances that drive Jones to the bottle for comfort, but the similarity in treatment of the theme and of the working-class characters is noticeable.

The Silver Box, like most nineteenth-century melodramas, has a strong narrative line and cannot be regarded only as a photographic study of a social *milieu*. The structure of the play relies perhaps rather too heavily on symmetry in order to make its point, one scene being carefully balanced with another. Within that symmetrical form, however, the social background of the characters is pictured in some detail, particularly regarding the use of properties. Many of these, associated with eating and drinking, serve to underline the contrasting lifestyles of the Barthwicks and the Joneses. Both scenes which involve the whole Barthwick family occur during, or immediately after, a meal. The 'political' discussion between Mr and Mrs Barthwick in Act I scene iii takes place at breakfast and is punctuated by reference to food. 'Cream?' 'Toast?' 'Now, John, eat your breakfast.' 'Tea, please.' Mrs Jones returns to her rented room with 'half a loaf, two onions, three potatoes, and a tiny piece of bacon'. She makes tea with 'powder which she pours from a screw of paper'. In the following scene the Barthwicks are finishing dinner, complaining about the quality of the nuts and passing the crackers, and more often the port, to Jack. The detective is offered sherry and sips it throughout his exchange with the family. Mrs Jones, except when she is being interrogated, is always working. In the first act, she is on her knees with a dustpan and brush: in the second, she is preparing a meal. The Barthwicks are always seen at leisure.

The naturalistic detail thus heightens the contrast between the families, as does the dialogue, for example, the words associated with drunkenness, with which both groups in rather different ways euphemistically deal. Mrs Jones refers to her husband as being 'not quite himself', a phrase which she also uses to describe Jack, when she discovers him on the sofa, but when pressed by the Magistrate, she asserts that Jones was 'almost quite drunk' on his return from his adventure at the Barthwicks. Jones says that he had "ad a drop to drink' but that Jack was 'drunk as a lord'. Jack describes himself as being 'a bit on' and later confesses to the Magistrates that he had 'too much champagne'. It is only the maid, Wheeler, who describes both Jack and Jones in the same words, 'tipsy like your husband. It's another kind of being out of work that drives him to drink.'

The characters are not caricatures of social types. The reason for the interpolation of the Livens' case at the beginning of the Police Court scene is to make the point that the unemployed are not only personified by the weak but rebellious Jones but also by the earnest and sober Livens. The play deals not with personifications of social types but with social attitudes. Galsworthy's description of his dramatis personae in his letter to Granville Barker about the casting confirms this, a remarkable document from one who was on his own admission a theatrical novice. He gives a clear throughline or 'keynote' as he called it for each character.[8] 'The keynote of *Barthwick* is *want of courage*. He thinks himself full of principle and invariably *compromises* in the face of facts.' As his wife acidly points out, 'Your principles are nothing but sheer fright.' He is prepared for a moment to tell the truth, but as soon as he

111

learns that Jack will have to appear in court, he retreats nervously. He is moved by the Livens' case and determines to speak in the House on the hardships of the unemployed, but refuses Mrs Jones's mute plea for help. His political theory is far distant from his social practice. 'The keynote of Mrs Barthwick is want of imagination', a lack which her husband points out, 'You can't imagine anything. You've no more imagination than a fly.' She is so moved by hearing the crying child outside the window, that she suggests withdrawing the prosecution, but the more immediate solution is to have the window shut. The circumstances behind the Jones's marriage, the plight of the unemployed and the political philosophy of the Labour Party are quite beyond her comprehension, 'They simply want what we've got.' Yet she, unlike her husband, sticks unflinchingly to her 'principles'. She is, according to Galsworthy, one of those 'hard-mouthed women' who are 'uncompromising and have courage.' 'The keynote of Jack is inherent want of principle derived from Barthwick and courage *by fits and starts* derived from Mrs Barthwick.' Jack, despite his continual attempts throughout the Police Court scene to draw attention to the parallels between his own plight and that of Jones, learns nothing. The last Stage Direction reads, '*Jack throwing up his head, walks with a swagger to the corridor.*'

The characters are believable enough, but any exploration of their innermost thoughts, motivations and backgrounds, such as one finds in Barker, is lacking. This lack may have been compensated for by the Court actors, whose earlier experience made them adept at presenting on stage psychologically realistic characters. In addition, Barker's forte as a director was his ability to create a 'real' environment on stage, peopled by 'real' characters. The realism of the piece and the absence of gratuitous stage effect were selected by critics as distinguishing features. 'When the author wrote it, he was thinking of life, not of the theatre',[9] wrote the critic of *The Bystander*, and A.B. Walkley in *The Times* compared the play favourably with Brieux's *Les Hannetons*. The acting was highly praised. 'As a drama which is full of real observation, Mr Galsworthy's piece, of course, gives fine scope to the actors at the Court' (*Illustrated London News*, 6 October 1906). This was most apparent in the Police Court scene. The small parts, the Relieving Offficer, the Magistrate's Clerk and the Usher were played not by inexperienced extras but by actors who had already established themselves as key members of the company, Edmund Gwenn, Lewis Casson and Norman Page. The Court 'no-stars' policy worked very much in Galsworthy's favour. For a novice to the fraught world of theatre Galsworthy found his experience at the Court, 'On the whole not quite so bad as I expected, but bad enough. None of one's personal conceptions quite realised – naturally.'[10] He attended several rehearsals and developed a great respect for Barker. In a letter to the director in 1926, Galsworthy wrote 'The English stage has produced a better school of acting than some, if not all, others partly, if not mainly thanks to you.'[11]

The play was very well received by the critics. *The Bystander* claimed that it would 'continually be quoted when the new school of dramatists is established', and the Court had once again demonstrated the wisdom of its policy to encourage men of letters to write for the stage.

Joy

'By George, how staggeringly different it is to *The Silver Box*', wrote Galsworthy to Garnett,[12] after he had submitted the script of *Joy* to Barker in February 1907. *Joy* was staged at the beginning of the ill-fated Savoy season in September, but the difference from Galsworthy's first play did not find favour with many critics, although his friends, Masefield and Conrad, found the piece more delicate in its observation and deeper in its character analysis.

The absence of a strong narrative line and, more importantly, of any social statement was one of the reasons for the disappointment felt by the theatrical avant-garde and the critics. The majority of the pioneers of the 'new drama', since the days of the Independent Theatre Society had been committed to social reform, and they found plays that failed to take an obviously critical stance on a social or moral question disconcerting to say the least.

There is very little plot. The scene is a country house belonging to Colonel and Mrs Hope. They have been entertaining Joy, the daughter of their niece, Molly Gwyn. Other guests are their daughter, Letty, and her husband Ernest Blunt. Molly's arrival is expected and eagerly awaited by her daughter who adores her, but Molly is accompanied by her lover, Maurice Lever. The nature of their relationship is suspected by the Hopes, and by Miss Beech, who has been governess to both Molly and Joy. Joy, who dislikes Lever and who has tried to close her eyes to the truth, is brought face to face with the fact that her mother cannot relinquish her relationship with her lover. Joy finds comfort and consolation in the love of Dick Merlon, and it is with the union of the two young people that the play ends.

Joy is subtitled, 'A play on the letter I', and the dominant theme is the overwhelming egotism, either overt or implicit, of all the characters, with the possible exception of Miss Beech, who, rather uncomfortably at times, functions as a commentator on the action. Egotism is not celebrated as in Shaw's plays, but, fairly gently, satirised. Each character acts primarily from motives of self-interest, and the pronouns, 'I', 'my' and 'mine' are used very frequently and as often as not underlined. There is perhaps even a play of words on 'mine' meaning 'belonging to oneself', and the gold 'mine' owned by Lever in which the Colonel and his wife are alternately anxious and reluctant to invest.

Characters are seen by one another as possessions. In the dispute about the outcome of the tennis match between himself and Ernest, the Colonel refuses to accept Letty's evidence because 'Letty's *your wife*.' Letty will not believe ill of Molly because 'She's *my own cousin*.' Joy cannot face the shame of Molly's affair because 'She's *my own mother*.' People are not seen as themselves but 'in relation to' the speaker.

The dramatic action underlines the theme. Characters often seem to be engaged in separate activities. For example, in the first scene, Mrs Hope is as absorbed in spraying roses as the Colonel is absorbed in his newspaper. Dick, hanging the Chinese lanterns at the beginning of Act II, is completely isolated from the Colonel and Lever who are engrossed in discussion about the mine.

The point that each individual sees himself or herself as 'a special case' is hammered home with less delicacy, most often through the rather unsatisfactory character of Miss Beech. Although the Colonel is 'as a rule' suspicious of investments in gold mines, he regards his own investment in Lever's as 'a special case' because *he* has studied the plans; although it is an accepted rule that one umpires one's own court in lawn tennis, the Colonel refuses to adhere to it 'in this case', because the rule lost him the match. Lever is at first unwilling to tell the Colonel about his reservations about the mine, lest it prejudice his chances with Molly. 'You can't act in a case like this as if you'd only a principle to consider – it's the special circumstances.' Although Dick would agree that 'as a rule' people so young should not enter into a serious relationship, Joy and Dick believe their love to be quite exceptional because *'It's you and me'*. These 'special cases' are for the most part dealt with humorously rather than critically. The harshest words come from the Colonel, moved to philosophy by the moonlight, 'By jove, Molly, I sometimes think we humans are a rubbishy lot – each of us talking and thinking of nothing but our own petty little affairs . . .'. But the characters are not unpleasant in their egotism. They are keenly observed but not harshly censored.

The relationship between Joy and her mother embodies the most acute case of egotism and that in which the results are potentially tragic. Edward Garnett disliked its 'sentimental intensity',[13] but it is the occasion for a most powerful scene between mother and daughter in the last act. Joy is in love with her mother, and dislikes Lever, not as himself, but as a threat to her intimate relationship with Molly. She is most anxious to be like her, hence the close questioning of Miss Beech about her mother's behaviour as a child. Miss Beech's answers sound a prophetic note, to which Joy is oblivious:

JOY: Peachey, duckie, what was Mother's *worst* fault?
MISS BEECH: Doing what she knew she oughtn't.
JOY: Was she ever sorry?
MISS BEECH: Yes, but she always went on doin' it.

Joy is eager to share a room with her mother, thus, of course, physically excluding Lever: she will not promise to dance with Dick, until she finds out whether or not her mother will dance with her. Unlike Molly, she puts the family relationship before the romantic one. She is also anxious that her mother will be the first person to see her with her hair up, that is, to see her as a woman, rather than

as a child. The intensity of her feelings makes her believe
that she has the right to be the sole possessor of her
mother's attention and her love. 'I would do anything for
you, mother', she blackmails. But her love does not give
her any understanding of Molly's loneliness and her need
for Lever.

Likewise Molly fails to understand, or at least to satisfy,
Joy's need for her. She sees Joy as a child, certainly at the
outset, and therefore as an extension of herself. 'You–are–
not a woman, Joy', she says cruelly. Joy, being 'an
untouched thing' with no experience of life, cannot imagine
Molly's predicament. The problem is that Galsworthy is
not totally clear in instructing the audience on how to read
Molly. She is not meant to be seen as a monster throwing
over her only and, for all practical purposes, fatherless
child for a lover, nor is she entirely upheld, as she would
have been in a play by Shaw or by Ibsen, as a heroine who is
quite justified in asserting her identity at the expense of her
daughter, or rather of a conventional stereotyped view of a
mother-daughter relationship.

MRS GWYN: D'you think – because I suffered when you
were born and because I've suffered with every ache
you ever had, that that gives you the right to dictate to
me now? (*In a dead voice*) I've been unhappy enough
and I shall be unhappy enough in the time to come.

Molly is also prepared to take the consequences of her own
actions. 'If it's wicked, *I* shall pay for it not *you*.' She is also
right when she tells Joy that her promise to devote herself
to her mother exclusively and for ever is an empty one,
made as a result of Joy's inexperience. 'There never has
been a woman, Joy, that did not fall in love.' Molly after all

resents Dick. But her own final choice of Lever is not seen as triumphant. She has lost Joy, who considers herself 'deserted', and the whole scene is conducted on a highly emotional level that lacks the cool objectivity of treatment found in Shaw. The only 'advice' proferred is from Miss Beech, 'There's suffering enough, without adding to it with our trumpery judgments', an indication that we are not being asked to condone or condemn, merely to accept and to try to understand.

The scenes between Molly and Joy make powerful theatre, and, of course Galsworthy was right when he refused to countenance a reconciliation between them. In a letter to Gilbert Murray, he wrote, 'The deep true ending of that situation comes once and for all at the moment when the mother and child find they are no longer first with one another. It would be no use patching it for the patch would not close the wounds.'[14]

Although the mother-daughter conflict is stated openly, and some of the other examples of egotism within the play are rather too crudely underlined, Galsworthy proves in *Joy* that he is also capable of the rather more subtle dramatic technique favoured by Barker, that is, the use of apparently inconsequential dialogue to demonstrate the inner working of characters and to create an atmosphere on stage. Much of the conversation in Act I is concerned with the allocation of rooms. This links with the egotism theme in that Ernest and Letty, in particular, do not want to give up *their* room, and that Mrs Hope sees all the rooms as *hers* to distribute as she pleases. But, in addition, as Dupont has pointed out, the obsessional discussion of sleeping arrangements hints at some sort of irregularity in sexual relationships that is lurking just below the surface, and the fact that it is the advent of Lever which causes the problem of the irritating re-allocation makes it clear that it is he who is the intruder in the house of Molly's relations, a house that has welcomed his main 'rival', Joy. His entry into Molly's world is difficult, inconvenient and embarrassing. The point is also made that a house ordered by Mrs Hope cannot accommodate everybody comfortably. A lover, in this case, Lever, is *de trop* in a conventional middle-class environment. Beneath what is on the surface a common-place domestic discussion, which at the same time becomes a running gag as Mrs Hope constantly changes her mind about how her visitors are to be distributed, there lie several layers of significance.

The setting of the play uses a naturalistic property, the hollow beech tree, as a symbolic centrepiece. The tree is a kind of magician's hat from which a variety of objects is pulled; in the first act the mundane objects such as the garden syringe and Dick's can of worms for fishing; in the last act, the irises which Dick picked for Joy and the champagne, presumably bought for Lever. There is a shift of emphasis in the properties, as in the theme, from the domestic and utilitarian to the romantic. Joy and Miss Beech (there is an obvious link in the name) are concealed by it, or in it, at the opening of the play, and Joy, by using the tree as a hiding place, learns that her mother is bringing Lever to the house, and later learns the truth about the relationship between them. What she learns both wounds and matures her. The tree is a Tree of Knowledge. At the end of the play, as Miss Beech watches Dick and Joy, linked together approaching the tree, she remarks, 'The blessed innocents.' There is a new Adam and Eve in the garden of Eden. In this context the tree can be either (or both) that of Knowledge and (or) of Life. The Tree of Life, as Miss Beech points out, divides Molly and Joy, the woman and the girl. The hollowness of the tree is highlighted, again by Miss Beech, 'We're all the same; we're all as hollow as that tree.' Such complex use of imagery was lacking in *The Silver Box*.

It would be wrong to claim for Galsworthy in this piece the subtle texture of dialogue and imagery that one finds in Barker, but he is reaching out towards a new technique, less heavy-handed than that of his first play, and *Joy* can be seen as a necessary preliminary to his two subsequent masterpieces, *Strife* and *Justice*.

Strife

Strife, the 'main idea' of which is that 'the sword perishes by the sword', was regarded by some critics as Galsworthy's finest play. It was first performed at the Duke of York's in March 1909. The piece had been written two years earlier, before the production of *Joy*, but had been rejected by several managements. The six matinées at the Duke of York's, directed by Barker, received considerable critical acclaim, and it was transferred to the evening bill at the Haymarket. In *Strife*, Galsworthy abandoned the discursive style employed in *Joy*, and returned to the technique that he had used successfully in *The Silver Box*, a symmetrical structure highlighting the contrast and conflict between classes and characters, which dictate both narrative and theme.

The 'strife' referred to in the title, is between the Board of Management of Tenartha Tin Plate works and the workers, who have been on strike for a long time. The strike is 'unofficial' as the Union refuses to support all the men's demands, and there is great hardship among the workforce and their families. The play, however, is not so much about the rights and wrongs of the strike as about the conflict between the leaders of each contesting party,

Roberts, the leader of the men, and Anthony, the Chairman of the Board.

The action takes place within a tight timescale. It begins at twelve noon and ends shortly after five o'clock. In the first scene, in the house of the Manager, Francis Underwood, Anthony's son-in-law, it is made clear that most of the members of the Board are anxious to reach a settlement with the men, either for reasons of self-interest, having regard to their falling dividends or out of humanitarian sympathy for the workers' suffering. Anthony stands firm. The leader of the striking workers, Roberts, is equally adamant, but in the course of the second act, set in Roberts' cottage and subsequently at an open air meeting, it becomes apparent that support for his policies is likewise dwindling. The men, for various reasons, the sorry state of their families, their own discomfort and conflicting beliefs, are anxious to settle with the Union. Roberts' oratory looks as though it will win the day, but his speech is interrupted by the news that his wife has died, and he leaves the platform. In the last act, again set in the Manager's house, Anthony, the Chairman of the Board is outvoted, and resigns. The leaderless workers and the Board without a Chairman agree terms, the same terms as had been drawn up by Harness, the Union official, and Tench, the Secretary of the Board, before the strike began. The play ends with a dialogue between Harness and Tench:

HARNESS: A woman dead; and the two best men broken.
TENCH (*staring at Harness – suddenly excited*): D'you
    know, sir – these terms, they're the *very same* we drew
    up together, you and I, and put to both sides before
    the fight began? All this – all this – and what for?

The answer to the question 'What for?' is perhaps difficult

for a modern audience, used to an overtly political propagandist theatre. Yet Galsworthy took pride in the apolitical nature of the piece, and in a letter to William Armstrong, director of the Liverpool Repertory Theatre, where the play was performed in 1911, he made clear his intention in writing *Strife*:

It has always been the fashion to suppose that it is a play on the subject of capital and labour. But the strike, which forms the staple material of the play, was chosen only as a convenient vehicle to carry the play's real theme, which is that of the Greek *uβpis* or violence. *Strife* is, indeed, a play on extremism or fanaticism . . .

He goes on to pride himself on the fact that contemporary representatives of Capital and Labour both saw fit to praise the work for its exposition of each political philosophy.

The case for Capital and the case for Labour are stated with equal passion and equal eloquence. Roberts expounds his philosophy in his speech to the vacillating and disputing workers at the meeting at the end of Act II: Anthony presents his views to the similarly divided Board in Act III. The two speeches although diametrically opposed in 'message' are very similar in the techniques of presentation employed, in their place in the dramatic structure and in the results they produce. Both men begin by citing personal experience to support their point of view:

ROBERTS: Don't I know that? Wasn't the work of *my* brains bought for seven hundred pounds and hasn't one hundred thousand pounds been gained them by that seven hundred without the stirring of a finger?

ANTHONY: I have had to do with 'men' for fifty years;

> I've always stood up to them; I have never been broken yet. I have fought the men of this Company four times, and four times I have beaten them.

Both speeches employ similar rhetorical devices, such as exclamation and repetition (ROBERTS: 'That's Capital!' and ANTHONY: 'Cant'): both use highly charged metaphorical language (ROBERTS: '. . . that white faced monster with the bloody lips that has sucked the life out of ourselves, our wives and children, since the world began', and ANTHONY: 'We *are* the machine; its brains and sinews', and 'deep in the bog of bankruptcy.') Both end by placing this particular conflict in the context of the general war between the forces of Capital and Labour, and each looks forward to a bleak future, were the opposing philosophy to triumph.

> ROBERTS: If we have not the hearts of men to stand against it [Capitalism] breast to breast, and eye to eye and force it backward till it cry for mercy, it will go on sucking life; and we shall stay forever what we are (*in almost a whisper*) less than the very dogs.

> ANTHONY: I am thinking of the future of this country, threatened with the black waters of confusion, threatened with mob government, threatened with what I cannot see. If by any conduct of mine I help to bring this on us, I shall be ashamed to look my fellows in the face.

The stage directions indicate that Galsworthy saw the two speeches as building in the same way. Roberts begins '*with withering scorn*', Anthony '*with ironical contempt*'. The immediate effect of both on their respective audiences is likewise similar. When Roberts concludes there is '*an utter stillness, and Roberts stands rocking his body slightly, with his eyes burning the faces of the crowd'. 'Anthony stares before him, at what he cannot see, and there is perfect stillness.'* Both men fail to rally support, although Roberts' defeat is largely occasioned by the news of his wife's death. Galsworthy went into some detail about how he saw this announcement affecting the workers in a letter to Edward Garnett (21 October 1907). [Roberts was called Williams in the early draft of the play.]

> . . . the news of Mrs Williams' (Roberts') death, being the crystallization of all the sufferings and fears that each man and his family have been through, acts like a red rag to them. They (after the first moment's hush of sympathy with Williams) feel sympathy with the dead woman, and show their resentment at Williams' leadership . . . and the application which each man makes of the fact to himself and his own family. That's the psychology of the crowd and it ought to be better brought out.

The fact of Annie Roberts' death also partly influences the outcome of the Board Meeting in the third act. Anthony makes reference to it immediately after his big speech on the necessity of maintaining the Capitalist economy, and thus it has the same place in the structure of the two scenes. It is his father's refusal to admit any responsibility for the tragedy that finally turns Edgar against him.

> ANTHONY: I am not aware that if my adversary suffer in a fair fight not sought by me, it is my fault.

Edgar's attack and the passion with which Anthony seeks to refute his son's arguments for corporate responsibility lead to his 'giddiness' immediately prior to his defeat. In an earlier draft of the play, Galsworthy considered a physical collapse, a stroke, for Anthony, but discarded the idea on the grounds that it was too melodramatic, and despite the very obvious parallelism in the structure, he was reluctant to have *two* physical collapses.

Galsworthy took great pains to present in as unbiased a manner as possible, both sides of the Capital *versus* Labour debate, using similar dramatic, structural and rhetorical devices to do so. His purpose is not to investigate two conflicting political philosophies but to examine the implacable conflict between two men, who are at once the heroes and the villains of the piece. They differ only in their social status and in their politics. Their determination (or obstinacy), their single-mindedness, their forcefulness (or violence) and their unshakable conviction in the rightness of the cause they support, show them to be brothers under the skin, a fact recognised by Enid, Anthony's daughter, and by his butler, Frost. As well as having marked similarities in their style of rhetoric, they both express themselves in the first Board meeting by the constant use of negatives. Anthony defies his Board with, 'No surrender', 'No compromise', 'No caving in'. In response to Harness's question, 'No concessions?' he replies, 'None.' Roberts' equally strong and positive views are likewise negatively expressed when he faces the Board:

> There's not one sentence of writing on that paper that we can do without. Not a single sentence.
> We are not so ignorant as you might suppose.
> Your position is not all that it might be – not exactly.

Their first sentences make clear not only the polarity of their views but their shared intense conviction in holding them:

ANTHONY: There can only be one master, Roberts.
ROBERTS: Then, by Gad, it'll be us.

Their first confrontation makes apparent their mutual respect. Roberts congratulates Anthony on 'knowing his own mind', as he knows his. When Underwood attempts to silence what is becoming a personal attack on the Chairman, Anthony, himself, gives Roberts licence to continue, 'Go on, Roberts, say what you like.' Just as Anthony refuses to take responsibility for the death of Roberts' wife – Roberts, it is clear, does not expect him to, and curtly dismisses Edgar's condolences with, 'Let your Father speak' – Roberts brushes aside Enid's plea to him to have regard to her father's age and state of health.

ROBERTS (*without raising his voice*): If I saw Mr Anthony going to die, and I could save him by lifting my hand, I would not lift the little finger of it.

At the final meeting, it is to Anthony that Roberts addresses himself, disregarding his own followers, the Union representative and the rest of the Board. Indeed it is to Anthony he appeals in his disgust at the outcome.

ROBERTS (*To Anthony*): But ye have not signed them terms. They can't make terms without their Chairman! Ye would never sign them terms! (*Anthony looks at him without speaking*) Don't tell me ye have! For the love o' God. (*with passionate appeal*) I counted on ye!

Roberts is human enough to feel satisfaction at his adversary's defeat although it has brought about his own, but a compassion inspired by the realisation of their mutual humilation at the hands of lesser men, leads him to say, '(*With a sudden dreadful calm*) So – they've done us both down, Mr Anthony?' The giants face each other, silent, broken but respectful.

> *Anthony rises with an effort. He turns to Roberts, who looks at him. They stand several seconds, gazing at each other fixedly; Anthony lifts his hand as though to salute, but lets it fall. The expression on Roberts' face changes from hostility to wonder. They bend their heads in token of respect . . .*

Had Galsworthy chosen to end the play with this visual image, the heroic stature of Roberts and Anthony would have been the final impression on the audience but the last exchange is between Harness and Tench after the defeated giants have exited. 'All this – all this – and – and what for?' – the common man's comment on the tragic heroes' *uβpis*.

Just as Galsworthy was careful to preserve the balance between the conflicting claims of Labour and Capital, he was equally careful in his attempt to balance the sympathy an audience might feel towards his two antagonists. Neither man is fortunate in his associates. The hero-villains tower over their respective followers. The Board Members are variously sleepy, self-absorbed and ineffectual. Their interests in the value of their shares is paramount. All regard a visit to Tenartha in February as inconvenient, uncomfortable and a nuisance. All lack the imagination to appreciate the workers' situation. The workers too present a fairly ineffectual picture in the early negotiations. Roberts, clearly, has a pretty poor opinion of their powers and silences them brusquely. In their jumbled, superstitious and ill-informed comments and in their pugnacious internal bickering, the workers provide a marked contrast to

Roberts in his self-sacrifice and his powerful rhetoric. Their performance before the Board at the end of the play is pitiful. Having abandoned Roberts as their spokesman and leader, they hand over their voice (and their souls?) to Harness and the Union. In his conversation with his wife Roberts makes explicit the contempt he feels, 'There's no heart in them, the cowards. Blind as bats, they are – can't see a day before their noses.'

Each opposing party has its female voice: on Anthony's side, his daughter, Enid Underwood, on Roberts', the firebrand, Madge Thomas, and in rather a different way, his wife, Annie. Madge and Enid have much in common. Both have the courage to enter the enemy's territory. Enid, albeit unfortunately clad in fur hat and jacket, braves Roberts in his home to bring help to Annie, and to plead with Roberts to agree to a settlement of the strike. Madge proudly enters the Underwood's drawing-room to announce Annie's death. Each receives a hostile reception, but bravely stands her ground. Both show themselves to be irked by having to conform to the passive feminine role expected of them by the men. Enid dismisses her father's advice to 'Read your novels, play your music, talk your talk', and resents the housewifely duties of providing firescreens, new pen-nibs and lunch for the all-male Board of which she wants to be a member. Madge too expresses impatience with woman's lot, 'Waiting an' waiting. I've no patience with it, waiting an' waiting – that's what a woman has to do.' As Madge waits for the outcome of the strikers' meeting, which she has attempted to influence by urging her father and her lover to turn against Roberts, Enid waits in the adjoining room as the Board Meeting proceeds. She, too, has attempted to influence the result in seeking to persuade Edgar to support their father. Madge's concern for her young brother is matched by Enid's protective snatching up of her baby's dress, '*as though it were the child itself*' in the face of Madge's incipient attack. Both women put the personal sufferings of their families before the issues of principle involved, for which Enid is reprimanded by her brother, 'Your family or yourself, and over goes the show.'

During her first encounter with her father, Enid makes the point that had he the benefit of her personal experience of the workers' situation, his attitude would change, although she does rather stress her own pain in witnessing their hardship and the uncomfortable position in which she and her husband find themselves. Her citing of Annie Roberts as a victim, however, does strike a chord. Anthony is sympathetic to an individual whom he knows and likes, if not to a class. He dismisses out of hand Enid's attestation that she does not believe in barriers between the classes. It is these barriers he asserts that protect her sentiments, her culture and her comforts. Enid's encounter with Annie, with Madge and with Roberts proves her father right, and exposes the fact that her apparent egalitarianism was never any more than sentimental phrase-making. Annie Roberts smiles at Enid's naïve assertion that the share-holders are really no better off than working men, since they 'have to keep up appearances' and 'pay rents and taxes'. The reality of Enid's deep-seated prejudice against the working-class becomes increasingly apparent. She believes that they drink and gamble, and if Roberts is different, that is because he is an engineer and 'not a common man'. Enid's attempt to play Lady Bountiful, as befits her cultural outlook, is sharply rebuffed by those she seeks to help, and her excursion across the class barriers, in which she earlier expressed disbelief, brings her over to her father's side. She admits to her brother, 'I don't feel half so sympathetic to them as I did before I went.'

The function and dramatic effect of the character of Annie Roberts is complex. On the one hand, her plight obviously wins sympathy for Roberts and the strike, since in her illness and death, the audience actually *sees* the effects of the hardship which have previously been described. Her conversation with Enid, Madge and her husband is punctuated by stage directions describing her constantly restless fingers, her painful attempts to breath and her feeble efforts to sit up. She is a brave and self-denying sufferer. But on the other hand, Roberts, as well as Anthony, is blamed for her death, not just by Enid, but by Madge, by Rous and by Thomas. Even his fellow-strikers lay her suffering at his door, and thus the balance of sympathy that might well have been upset by this character is maintained.

The balance Galsworthy effects throughout is exemplified in Annie's speech to Enid on the lot of the working man. She begins by quoting Roberts, '(*with a sort of excitement*) Roberts says a working man's life is all a gamble, from the time 'e's born to the time 'e dies. He says, M'm, that when a working man's baby is born, it's a toss up from breath to breath whether it ever draws another and so on all 'is life; an' when he comes to be old, it's the workhouse or the grave. He says that without a man is very near, and pinches and stints 'imself and 'is children to save, there can't be neither surplus nor security.' This simple and moving speech cannot fail to win sympathy for Roberts, but she goes on, and the stage direction stresses '*the personal feeling of the last words*', 'That's why he wouldn't have no children (*she sinks back*) not though I *wanted* them.' This is the uncomplaining woman's only complaint. While explicitly enlisting the audience's sympathy for Roberts she at the same time exposes his inhumanity.

Frost, Anthony's manservant, has a similar function

vis-à-vis his master. He fusses over the old man and appears to have genuine concern for his welfare thus showing the audience that Anthony is capable of inspiring loyalty in his servants. But Frost also exposes the hero-villain as someone who can be 'handled' or 'yumoured' with a little bit of tact. He confides in Enid,

> I'm sure if the other gentlemen were to give up to Mr Anthony, and quietly let the men 'ave what they want afterwards, that'd be the best way. I find that very useful with him at times, M'm.

It is Frost who describes both Anthony and Roberts as 'violent' – 'violence' being Galsworthy's translation of the Greek '*υβρis*'.

There is no easy solution to the problems posed by *Strife*. Neither a Capitalist nor a Labour orientated political philosophy is advocated. The hero-villains are seen as fine men who bring pain and misery to their dependants and relations. The pragmatists lack backbone and vision. The symmetrically balanced structure, employed somewhat crudely in *The Silver Box*, is now used more subtly to expose more subtle differences in the antagonists and in the classes they, in part, represent. Rather than showing 'a critical and dissenting attitude towards contemporary codes of morality', *Strife* presents an incident that exposes, rather than attacks, some of the causes of industrial unrest and of personal tragedy.

Justice

If *Strife* eschewed propagandism, *Justice* might be seen as the propagandist play *par excellence* for its production was instrumental in bringing about a change in the law relating to solitary confinement in prisons. Galsworthy had for a long time been committed to penal reform, and in particular he sought to curtail the length of time prisoners spent in solitary confinement. In 1907, he had visited Dartmoor, and his horror at the distress among prisoners so confined is expressed in *The House of Silence* and *Order*. By the time the play was written he had also visited Pentonville Prison, Lewes Gaol and Chelmsford Gaol, and had personally interviewed over sixty prisoners. By dint of a great deal of political lobbying and an Open Letter to the Home Secretary, Herbert Gladstone, he was influential in achieving a reduction of the time spent in solitary confinement. 'No one who hasn't seen and through seeing felt with those poor creatures, can tell what incalculable misery it will remove', he wrote to Mrs Scott in December 1909,[15] but the reforms had not gone far enough. The next initiative in the campaign was *Justice*, which received two simultaneous first productions, by Barker at the Duke of York's Theatre as part of Frohman's Repertory Season, and at the Glasgow Repertory Theatre, on 21 February 1910.

Justice, as befits its title, opens in the office of a firm of solicitors, James and Walter How. One of the clerks, a young man named Falder, has forged a cheque to get enough money to emigrate with the woman he loves, Ruth Honeywill, who is married to a drunken and violent man. The forgery is discovered and after much debate between James How, his son, Walter, and their managing clerk, Cokeson, it is agreed that Falder must be prosecuted for his crime. The second act shows Falder's trial. The Defence Counsel tries to persuade the Court that Falder was temporarily insane. Cokeson, Ruth Honeywill and Falder give evidence, which seems to prove that, if not actually *insane*, he was certainly in a highly disturbed state of mind, 'jumpy', as Cokeson puts it. This is not felt to be enough to excuse him. the Prosecution stresses that Falder subsequently altered the counterfoil in the chequebook to conceal his crime and, in addition, the irregularity of his relationship with Ruth counts against him. He is sentenced to three years' penal servitude.

In Act III, Cokeson, who is concerned about Falder, visits the Prison Governor. He tries to impress on the Governor and on the Prison Doctor and Chaplain that the period of solitary confinement that he is undergoing might well damage Falder's physical and psychological health, but he is assured that Falder is being carefully watched, and that there are no abnormal signs of distress. His request that Ruth be allowed to visit the prisoner is refused. The second scene takes place in the cell block. Several prisoners, including Falder, are interviewed by the Governor, who is shown to be sympathetic and humane, but intent on doing the job which the Law requires of him. The short third scene, without any dialogue, shows the mental agony which Falder is suffering in solitary confinement. The boredom and the silence, the darkness and then the sudden bright light are clearly affecting his mind.

A sound from far away, as of distant, full beating on thick metal, is suddenly audible. Falder shrinks back, not able to bear this sudden clamour. But the sound grows, as though some great tumbril were rolling towards the cell. And gradually it seems to hynotize him. He begins creeping inch by inch nearer to the door. The banging sound, travelling from cell to cell, draws closer and closer; Falder's hands are seen moving as if his spirit had already joined in this beating, and the sound swells till it seems to have entered the very cell. He suddenly raises his clenched fists. Panting violently, he flings himself at his door, and beats on it.

It was the effect of this scene particularly that motivated the new Home Secretary, Winston Churchill, to seek a further modification in the Law.

The last act, once again set in the solicitors' office, takes place two years later, and opens, as did the first act, with a scene between Cokeson and Ruth, who has left her brutish husband and has been forced by poverty to become a prostitute. She has, however, just met Falder, now on parole from prison and 'sleeping rough' in the park, and has come to the solicitors' office to plead for his reinstatement as a clerk. Cokeson and the partners are sympathetic. James's reservations about Ruth are dispelled when it is made clear that she now has grounds for divorce, and that she and Falder could eventually marry. Cokeson, however, feels that he must reveal that Ruth has been living on immoral earnings. She agrees with James that she must give up any hope of continuing her relationship with Falder. The police officer who arrested Falder in Act I enters in search of him, as he has failed to report to the police, a condition of his parole. The partners and Cokeson refuse to say that he is in the next room, but the detective discovers him. Falder, faced with another term in prison, and the loss of Ruth, jumps (or falls) out of the window and is killed.

The London production of *Justice* was seen not only by Churchill but also by Sir Evelyn Ruggles-Brise, the Head of the Police Commission. A whole programme of penal reform was implemented, including a further reduction of the period spent in solitary confinement. The fact that Churchill felt that Galsworthy's play was an important factor in the decision to effect the reforms is demonstrated by his communicating his plans to Galsworthy prior to their announcement in Parliament. Rarely has a piece of dramatic writing had such an immediate and positive result. 'How much greater it is to have saved a lot of men and women from two months' solitary confinement than to have sent any number of over-fed audiences into raptures', wrote Gilbert Murray.[16]

Yet despite Galsworthy's satisfaction that his play had advanced a cause dear to his heart, it is clear from his later letters that he felt the emphasis placed on the propagandist aspect of the work rather distorted his real purpose. 'The public . . . take it for a tract on solitary confinement (which incidentally it was – but only incidentally).'[17] He saw the play as being, 'the non-ephemeral presentment which it gives of the – perhaps inevitable – goring to death of the weak and sick members of the herd by the herd as a whole.'[18] The 'main idea' was that Justice was a blind goddess in the hands of man – quite unable to make the punishment fit the crime.

Galsworthy subtitled the play 'A Tragedy', and it was to achieve the tragic catharsis, in his own words 'the pure emotion of something elemental', that he chose, after much debate, to end the play with Falder's death. Barker would have preferred the curtain to come down after the re-arrest, and Galsworthy was sufficiently persuaded to prepare an alternative ending. He sent both versions to Gilbert Murray for comment. Murray's reply is illuminating not only with regard to *Justice*, but also about the conventions of the 'new drama' movement, of which he was such a staunch supporter:

Your play is not a Blue Book – a tract: it is a tragedy. And to cut the death because it is not relevant to the Prison System would be to treat it like a tract. Remember that H.G.B. [Barker] has a curious dislike for great and direct passion, and for elemental things . . . Also, remember this: That our modern dramatic movement, with all its great qualities, has had this great lack. It has, on the whole, not reached – it has not really attempted – the great motives or the sublime kinds of tragedy. I should not wonder if nearly all our Court Theatre set blamed you for Falder's death and 'Gentle Jesus', but I should feel clear that they were wrong – they were in the bonds of their own orthodoxy.[19]

Murray's comment on Barker is harsh in that it does not appear to take account of the latter's achievement in *Waste*, which, possibly more successfully than *Justice*, marries political criticism with personal tragedy. It does, however, raise the interesting theoretical question of the extent to which a play, designed, (at least in part, according to the author himself) to rectify a *particular* social evil can rise to the status of tragedy. Barker clearly felt, in the event mistakenly, that the death of Falder would result in a diminution of the play's effect as propaganda, and it would become the sad tale of one unfortunate individual. Galsworthy and Murray, however, were both agreed that Falder's death was an artistic necessity, giving the play its status as 'tragedy'. Falder is, however, no classical tragic hero. He is acknowledged by all to be lacking in strength of character and in physical and mental robustness. In the stage directions, words such as 'pale', 'scared' and 'irresolute' are used to describe him. Galsworthy saw him as 'a weak and sick member of the herd'. He is sensitive, selflessly devoted to Ruth and fundamentally honest, as haunted by guilt as by fear of discovery, but his death does not inspire that sense of waste of something potentially exceptional or splendid that one expects from the death of a 'tragic hero', or for that matter one experiences in the 'new drama' after the suicides of Hedda Gabler or Henry Trebell. The effect Galsworthy seems to be seeking is rather one of *relief* – Murray called it 'artistic' relief – that

Falder has finally 'escaped'.

Critics have seen the weakness of Falder as the weakness of the play, both as a tragedy and a piece of propaganda. But, as far as the propagandist aspect of the play is concerned Galsworthy shows that a period in solitary confinement has dangerous results, not only on a weak and unstable character like Falder, but on tough old lags, like Moaney, Clipton and O'Cleary, all of whom are described in some detail. Each has his own way of attempting to deal with his period in solitary. Moaney has spent five weeks laboriously sawing through a bar in his cell, partly to keep his hand in pending his release, partly to pass the time. So bored is he, that he rejects the Governor's offer to overlook his offence if he promises not to repeat it. 'I must have something to interest me.' Clipton finds refuge in sleep, ('the only comfort I've got in here'), a direct quote from one of the prisoners interviewed by Galsworthy, and O'Cleary, in banging on his cell door. The task of making rush matting, as he says, 'don't take the brains of a mouse'. All are disturbed by the tedium and the silence of life in their solitary cells. Falder's distress is in no way exceptional, and it is not seen to be so by the Prison Doctor:

> THE DOCTOR: Well, I don't think the separate's doing him any good; but then I could say the same of a lot of them – they'd get on better in the shops, there's no doubt.
>
> THE GOVERNOR: You mean you'd have to recommend others?
>
> THE DOCTOR: A dozen at least.

'*The Law, is what it is*', says the Judge, 'a majestic edifice, sheltering all of us, each stone of which rests on another.' Yet the Law is flawed, because it cannot deal with Falder who is truly 'a special case'. The process, begun by James How's decision to prosecute, carries on with relentless logic until it results in Falder's death. The clerk, Sweedle, points out that his process might have been stopped at several points: 'The governor made a mistake – if you ask me', he confides to Ruth, 'He ought to have given him a chanst. And, *I* say, the judge ought to ha' let him go after that.' Cokeson, too, makes an unsuccessful attempt to arrest events with his 'Here! Here! What are we doing?' after Falder's exit with the detective. The rest of the play answers his question – a man is brought into conflict with Justice, an institution as 'blind' and as unbending as the Fates. When Falder has been sentenced, the second act ends with the call for 'the next case', a sensitively used device to indicate the unrelenting processes of the Law.

It is made clear throughout the play that it is the 'process of Justice' which destroys Falder, not the malpractice of the individuals involved in it. James How, in insisting on prosecution, puts forward the rational view that a known forger cannot remain an employee of a respectable firm of solicitors, nor can a man who has given in to temptation be let loose on an unsuspecting world where he might well commit a similar crime if put under emotional pressure. James is willing to reinstate Falder when he has 'paid his debt to society', and he protects him against police pressure. The Prosecuting Counsel with some justification exposes the flaws in the Defence's plea of temporary insanity. The staff of the Prison, the Governor, the Doctor, the Chaplain and the Warden are humane enough within their acknowledged responsibilities. *Justice*, although similar to Tom Taylor's *Ticket-of-Leave Man* in certain narrative aspects, is quite different in that Taylor, in true melodramatic fashion, firmly attributes blame to individual villains. The inviolable *rightness* of British justice is never questioned, although, technically Taylor's hero, Bob Brierly, is innocent of the forgery for which he is imprisoned, and the Law is plainly wrong to convict him. Prison makes 'a man' of Bob Brierly, but a physical wreck of Falder. At the end of Taylor's play both the victim of Justice and Justice itself are vindicated. Galsworthy's conclusion exposes the flaws in the Law and the weakness of its victim. Melodrama personifies and particularises the source of evil: Galsworthy, by contrast, shows well-meaning and high-principled individuals becoming cogs in an inexorable machine. The machine of justice with its 'rolling chariot wheels' rather than any individual in its service, is shown to be inflexible and, therefore, inhumane.

One of the most blatant prejudices is related to the moral, rather than the legal, question of the relationships between men and women. What Cokeson terms 'extenuating circumstances' (Falder's love of Ruth and his desire to remove her from her husband's brutality), James How calls 'dissolute habits'. The Judge in his cross-examination of Ruth is, at the very least, disapproving of her attitude to her husband:

> JUDGE: You say your married life is an unhappy one? Faults on both sides?
> RUTH: Only that I never bowed down to him. I don't see why I should, sir, not to a man like that.
> JUDGE: You refused to obey him?

The subtext of the last question is clearly admonitory. His moral rigidity is further demonstrated in his speech prior to passing sentence, 'She is a married woman, and the fact is patent that you committed this crime with a view to furthering an immoral design.' The Governor refuses Ruth access to Falder, because she is not his wife and the renunciation of Ruth is a condition of Falder's reinstatement as a clerk in James How's office. In the eyes of James and of Cokeson, her having lived as a 'kept woman' debars her from remarriage. The relationship between Falder and Ruth is 'pure' in that it has never been consummated, and the love each bears for the other gives stature to both, yet it is one of the main reasons for the harshness of the sentence.

Ruth is as much a victim of the mechanistic aspects of Justice as Falder. As Frome, the Defence Counsel makes clear, 'another offence besides violence is necessary to enable a woman to obtain a divorce.' Only when she is turned out of the marital home does she have the necessary grounds. Her recourse to prostitution is the result of her inability to support her children by sewing shirts, the same task which Falder is set in prison. Her 'imprisonment' in poverty is thus compared to his period in solitary, and her 'dissolute habits', like Falder's, are synonymous with 'extenuating circumstances'. The Law fails Ruth as it failed Falder, not through the villainy of its various officers, but ironically through its celebrated 'blindness'.

Galsworthy saw the main artistic conception behind the play as being a picture of the true proportions between offence and punishment as opposed to *blind* Justice. The pride that the legal profession takes in being no respecter of persons is, in his view, misplaced. *Legally*, the Judge is right to instruct the Jury, 'You must not allow any considerations of age or temptation to weigh with you in finding your verdict', but *morally*, old Cokeson is right to emphasise the 'extenuating circumstances' that led to temptation. The 'blindness' of the judicial system is for Galsworthy an extension of the blindness, or the lack of imagination, of the individuals in its service. As Cokeson says, 'Of course, what you don't see doesn't trouble you; but I don't want to have him on my mind.' When Walter

How begs his father to put himself in Falder's place, the reply is uncompromising, 'You ask too much of me.' As in *Strife*, the son pleads for mercy as the father upholds justice. The Prison authorities are satisfied that Falder has put on weight during his spell in gaol. What he has lost mentally and spiritually, or as he puts it 'in his head' and 'in his heart' is not seen, not quantifiable, and, therefore disregarded. The 'blindness' of the Goddess of Justice is not, then, for Galsworthy a positive attribute, and once again in this work, his plea is for sympathy, for understanding and for imagination.

The character who marries the propagandist theme, that tolerance and imagination can help mankind to adapt its institutions to serve its weakest members, and the tragic theme, that Justice is a relentless Fate, striking weak and strong alike in its blindness, is Cokeson, the managing clerk in the solicitors' office. Cokeson describes himself on more than one occasion as 'the plain man'. He is good at his work and enjoys it. He is fond of dogs, and with his 'honest dog face' resembles one. He is concerned that his dinners should be hot and that 'a jolly atmosphere' prevail in the office. His staunch belief in the Law which he has served for many years, is matched by his deep and unquestioning religious faith. While his sense of propriety is outraged that Ruth should presume to visit Falder at the office – and a *lawyer's* office at that – his humanity allows them a minute of private conversation. His presentation to Falder of a tract on 'Purity in the Home' is ironic. Neither the accepted canons of the Church nor of the Law can deal with Falder's situation. The impetus to mercy, characterised by Walter How, and the impetus to Justice, characterised by James, are constantly at war within Cokeson in the first scene, and he is, therefore, for the audience a key to the debate within the play. He truly believes that, 'We shan't want to set ourselves up against the law', but does not want Falder, struggling 'with flesh and the devil' to be sent to prison, a 'narsty' place. Reluctant always 'to set himself up' against authority he still makes his plea to the Prison Governor to take special care of the 'eurotic' Falder. His deeply held belief in the legal process has its comic side, too, in his misuse of legal jargon, 'sign qua nonne' and 'prime facey', and in his assiduous efforts to avoid hearsay evidence during his cross-examination. The 'plain man' is given the last word in Act I, the question, 'What are we doing?' – a question directed to himself, to those involved in the starting up of 'the rolling wheels of the chariot of Justice' and to the audience. At the end he is used again to direct the audience's feeling, to evoke the 'artistic relief' that Galsworthy sought, with his benediction, 'No one'll touch him now! Never again! He's safe with gentle Jesus.' It is little wonder that Murray saw the concluding line as causing problems for the sophisticated, politically aware and probably fashionably agnostic audience for the 'new drama'. Galsworthy, in a letter to W.L. George, indicated that the last line was in fact designed to evoke a rather sour or at least ironic response. '*Justice* tried to paint the picture of how the herd (in crude self-preservation) gore to death its weak members – with the moral of how jolly consistent that is with a religion that worships "Gentle Jesus"'.[20] He was also apprehensive about the character in performance but was fortunate in that Barker was able to cast Edmund Gwenn, an actor well able to combine comedy with 'real feeling', for the conflict in Cokeson's mind is the conflict of the play in microcosm.

In *Justice*, more than in any of his earlier plays, Galsworthy masters the subtle marriage of naturalistic detail and 'delicate' symbolism, an art of which Ibsen was a masterly exponent. Each of the stage settings is described in some detail – *the well-worn mahogany and leather'* of Cokeson's office; *'the foggy October day in the Courtroom';* *'the greenish distemper up to a stripe of deeper green'* of the Prison corridor; and, above all, Falder's cell, where the precision was no doubt the result of personal experience:

> *Falder's cell, a whitewashed space thirteen feet broad by seven feet deep, and nine feet high, with a rounded ceiling. The floor is of shiny blackened bricks. The barred window, with a ventilator, is high up in the middle of the end wall. In the middle of the opposite end wall is the narrow door.*

Yet none of these locations exists only as an appropriate *milieu* for the characters within it. Each, in addition, symbolises a part of the inexorable process of Justice – from solicitors' office, to courtroom, to the administrative offices of the Prison, to the Prison corridor, to an individual cell. The theme is dramatised in the settings.

The two lawyers are likewise described in naturalistic terms. Frome, Falder's Defence Counsel is 'a young, tall man, clean-shaven in a very white wig': Cleaver, the Counsel for the Crown, is 'a dried yellowish man, of more than middle age, in a wig worn almost to the colour of his face'. Since Frome is a young man, less experienced in the Law, it is, in naturalistic terms, correct that his wig should be newer and therefore 'whiter', than Cleaver's. Yet the contrast exists on another level. Frome deliberately seeks, as Cleaver says, to 'get round the Law' in bringing to the Court's attention the stress that motivated Falder's crime. He takes a fresh approach and makes a covert plea for Mercy. Both Cleaver and his wig have been well-used in the service of the Law, and, stressing the gravity of the offence, he demands Justice.

The Prison Governor wears a glove because two fingers of one hand are missing. This might be seen as a largely superfluous naturalistic detail to fill out a character who has personally experienced some unknown physical misfortune. It might also be seen as a comment on the 'even-handedness' or otherwise of Justice. The principal officer of the Prison is maimed, as is the system under which he operates.

Galsworthy has been criticised for introducing details into his stage directions that cannot possibly be read by an audience, a typical lapse of the novelist turned dramatist, according to Dupont. The audience is not going to see that the open book in Falder's cell is *Lorna Doone*, nor be aware of the patterns made by the prisoners in the exercise yard below the Governor's window. But Galsworthy may have been more a dramatist writing for actors than Dupont admits. The actor playing Falder will be helped in building his character by knowing the title of the book, and, one feels that if Galsworthy had not supplied it in his stage directions, Granville Barker would have done so in rehearsals. It is not the sight of the prisoners taking exercise that affects the audience but Cokeson's reaction to it. It helps the actor to envisage the scene if it is described. Very seldom are Galsworthy's details irrelevant to the creation of the environment and atmosphere of the scene.

In at least two instances, Galsworthy places his characters in positions on the stage, which are perfectly acceptable in naturalistic terms, but which also help the audience to understand the conflict between or within them and their attitudes. In the Courtroom, it is naturalistically correct that the accused faces the Judge, but on stage, courtrooms can be presented from any angle. Galsworthy takes great pains to stress that '*Falder is sitting exactly opposite to the Judge*'. The 'special case' is put in direct physical opposition to the supreme representative of the Law. He further describes the Judge as 'raised above the clamour of the court, unconscious of and oblivious to everything'. The inequity of the ensuing conflict and the distance between Justice and 'the people' are thus expressed in physical terms. In the last act, when Ruth is brought into the office to hear the partners' decision on Falder's reinstatement, she and Falder stand together on one side of the room, James, Walter and Cokeson, on the other. This direct confrontation which is held for a while in silence is broken by Cokeson who turns to his desk to sort through papers. It also shows Cokeson's inner dilemma and his unwillingness to be aligned with either party. Physically and ideologically, he breaks ranks.

In terms of gesture as well as in his use of physical topography, Galsworthy employs a 'delicate' symbolism. The act of charging Falder with felony which sets events in motion is effected almost entirely by signs, rather than by words. James gives the cashier, who has identified Falder, 'an interrogative look'. He replies with a nod. It is 'a sign from James' that makes the detective lay hands on his prisoner, and a motion of his hand that dismisses Falder's plea for mercy. James is a man of few words who dislikes things to 'descend into talk' but the use of gesture here additionally gives the effect of an implacable force at work of which the man is only an instrument. Galsworthy's use of stage technique is masterly and extends far beyond the limitations of photographic naturalism. While losing none of the precise detail necessary to create the illusion of reality, he makes those very details reveal and enhance the presentation of meaning.

Justice opened the Frohman Repertory Season at the Duke of York's. Barrie had been most anxious that Galsworthy complete the play in time and his faith was justified, for the piece was a considerable financial success. In Glasgow, where it was directed by Lewin Mannering, with due acknowledgement to the help given by Barker, it was equally well received. The casts of both productions included members of the former Court company. Barker had felt on reading the play that it was not a difficult one to cast. He found an excellent Falder in Dennis Eadie, a fine character actor rather than a regular *jeune primeur*. The part of Falder, according to the critic of *The Daily Telegraph* (22 February 1910) required 'a capable actor full of quick sensitive perception, sympathetic manner, clever suggestiveness and a large amount of sheer histrionic skill'. All these qualities Eadie displayed. Cokeson, the part that had concerned Galsworthy, was played by Edmund Gwenn, a regular Court actor, whose most famous character had been 'Enery Straker in *Man and Superman*. Like Eadie, he had appeared in *The Silver Box*, in a small part. Edyth Olive, whose casting as Ruth worried Galsworthy lest she proved to be 'too classical and exotic; had made her name in Barker's production of Gilbert Murray's translations of Euripides. She had also, however, taken the part of Honor in *The Voysey Inheritance*, and had therefore experience in working in the 'naturalistic' drama. Galsworthy's fears were groundless for it was felt that she managed to combine 'truth to life' with 'a tragic quality'. In Glasgow the part of Ruth was taken by Irene Rooke, who had created the role of Mrs Jones in *The Silver Box* at the Court.

Barker's production was highly regarded especially for his handling of the Courtroom Scene, but it might well have been Barker's flair for naturalistic presentation that led critics to label Galsworthy's work 'photographic'. P.P. Howe wrote, 'The Court scene was indeed put on with a masterly hand by Mr Barker. It was so good as to raise the whole question of dramatic realism. One might just as well have been in a court of law: and some will say when we go out after dinner for pleasure we had sooner go elsewhere.'[21] The reviewer of the Glasgow Repertory production in *The Glasgow News* (22 February 1910) seems to indicate that this presentation penetrated beneath the surface naturalism to the core of the play as Galsworthy himself saw it. 'Modern realism', he wrote, 'while aiming at as much external verisimilitude as will satisfy the eye, is concerned mainly with spiritual verities . . . Galsworthy is a dramatist first and a social reformer afterwards' – a concluding verdict on his work against which the writer would lodge no appeal.

3
St John Hankin

Hankin is, of all the Court dramatists, the one who is most closely allied to Shaw in his open revolt against contemporary theatre practice. He believed that as a result of increased commercialism and of the resultant pandering to middle-class taste, the drama had been 'reduced to the last stage of intellectual decrepitude'. He espoused the cause of the Stage Society, believing that whether or not the plays it presented were masterpieces, they were at least not merely conventional hack-work. From 1902 until his death he served on the Society's Council of Management, and his first full length play, *The Two Mr Wetherbys* was staged by the Society in 1903. This is a much slighter piece than his later works, but the opposing philosophies of the 'good', but unhappy, Mr Wetherby and of his joyful brother, who is 'bad' according to the dictates of social convention, give rise to some humour and much irony. The Society also staged his translation of Brieux's *The Three Daughters of M. Dupont*, which was later published in an edition of three plays by Brieux, with a Preface by Shaw.

St John Hankin was born in Southampton in 1869. After he had completed his education at Malvern Public School, he went to Merton College, Oxford, and on graduating, began a journalistic career. He wrote for the *Saturday Review*, and following a short stay in India, returned to

Britain, to work for two years (1897–99) as a drama critic for *The Times*. During this period he also contributed a series of articles to *Punch*, including *Dramatic Sequels* to famous plays, such as *Caste* and *A Doll's House*. These demonstrate Hankin's keen sense of humour and his critical acuity and were published in one volume in 1901.

By 1905, he had virtually given up journalism to devote himself to playwriting. The Court Theatre presented two of his plays, *The Return of the Prodigal*, 1905, and 1907, and *The Charity that began at Home*, 1906. The Stage Society produced *The Cassilis Engagement* in 1907, and *The Last of the De Mullins* in 1908. Although Hankin died before the Censorship issue came to a head in the appointment of the Select Committee in 1909, he contributed to the debate with an excellent essay entitled 'Puritanism and the Theatre', published in the *Fortnightly Review* in 1906.

In 1909, fearing the onset of the crippling disease that had left his father helpless, he drowned himself at Llandrindod Wells in Wales, as Shaw said, 'a death straight out of *Ghosts*'. In his Obituary, he called Hankin 'a most gifted writer of high comedy of the kind that is a stirring and important criticism of life.'

The Return of the Prodigal

The Return of the Prodigal is a modern gloss on the biblical parable. Eustace Jackson, the prodigal of the title, returns to his prosperous middle-class home in the village of Chedleigh, having squandered the portion of £1,000 with which his father had dispatched him to Australia some years previously. In Hankin's version, the prodigal is unrepentant (his melodramatic 'walk' from London to his home was accomplished with the help of the railway), and no fatted calf is killed for him. His devoted mother, used to helping lame ducks, extends a welcome, but his father, deeply involved in procuring for himself a seat in the House of Commons, and his hard-working and materialistic brother, Henry, find Eustace's presence in the household both an irritant and an embarrassment. Mr Jackson is convinced that an indigent son, who, if evicted from the family home, threatens to take up residence in the local workhouse or to attempt suicide in the local canal, would put paid to his political ambitions. Henry realises that his prospects of marriage with the aristocratic Stella Faringford would founder. Eustace suggests a solution, that his father make him a generous annual allowance, in return for which he promises to stay away. Mr Jackson and Henry agree (with regrets over the loss of money rather than of Eustace), and the 'Prodigal' exits with his first instalment of the annual allowance of £250. For an additional £50 a year, he promises not to write.

In this interpretation of the story, Hankin not only reverses the 'message' of the parable, but also uses it as a peg on which to hang his social criticism. This is sometimes comic, as in his ironic comments on the medical profession, and sometimes very serious both in his indictment of middle-class materialism and opportunism and in his implicit demand for a reassessment of the accepted role of women in society.

Eustace, like his father and his brother, preys on fellow members of society, although he alone has self-awareness enough to realise it.

> They're [Mr Jackson and Henry] very much like me. We belong to the predatory type. Only they're more successful than I am. They live on their workpeople. I propose to live on them.

Earlier the Jackson family has been shown as being obsessed with the profit motive and with material well-being. Their drawing room, which is 'too full of everything' shows in its busy materialism, 'opulence rather than taste'; the installation of electric light enables the mill to be used all round the clock; a new path from the house to the mill saves Henry time in getting to work; improved machinery means higher profits, although not better cloth; Henry seeks to marry Stella for social advancement, not for love; Mr Jackson's election campaign is not supported by deeply held principles, but by continual compromises to win the support of as many vested interests as possible, exemplified by his uneasy wooing of both the Temperance movement and the Licensed Victuallers.

A social system, that is by its nature exploitative breeds exploiters and parasites. It is on the Jacksons' ambitions, encouraged by their wealth, that Eustace preys. As he makes clear to Henry, 'Luckily the governor's political ambitions and your social ambitions gave me the pull over you, and I used it.' In twentieth–century society, the Prodigal is not welcomed with love but dismissed with hush money. The whole structure of such a society, as Lady Faringford says, in a speech that is more than a little out of character for its perception if not for its élitism, is built on a conspiracy of silence.

We were born into this world with what is called position. Owing to that position we are received everywhere, flattered, made much of. Though we are poor, rich people are eager to invite us to their houses and marry our daughters. So much the better for us. But if we began telling people that position was all moonshine, family an antiquated superstition, and many duchesses far less like ladies that their maids, the world would ultimately discover that what we were saying was perfectly true. Whereupon we should lose the very comfortable niche in the social system which we at present enjoy, and – who knows? – might actually be reduced in the end to doing something useful for our living like other people. No, no, my dear, rank and birth and the peerage MAY be all nonsense, but it isn't OUR business to say so.

Doctor Glaisher silently acquiesces to the lie of Eustace's collapse to conceal his own ignorance of medicine, and thus tacitly aids Eustace to dupe his family.

The Prodigal is not the only weak vessel whose plight is touched on in the play. Violet, Eustace's sister, is used by her family and is also a victim of their social climbing. Both Henry and Eustace treat her as a servant, expecting her to pour their coffee and generally administer to their needs. Her father treats her not as a grown woman with interests of her own, but as a child, 'That's a good girl', he says patronisingly, as she fetches his hat and stick. As far as marriage prospects are concerned, she is caught in the same dilemma as the Huxtable girls in *The Madras House*, having neither enough money of her own nor sufficient rank to make a 'good' marriage, but having too much money and position to marry any of 'the little people' as she calls them, who are now almost forbidden the house. Since the idea of her taking up any kind of employment is unthinkable, she remains a prisoner in the over-upholstered Jackson household. It is touching that the cheap novel she is reading is called *Hester's Escape*. Whereas Eustace exploits the exploiters, Violet remains their victim, sewing for church bazaars and playing the piano for the unappreciative ears of Lady Faringford. The importance that Hankin attributed to the speech in which Violet explains her problem to

Eustace is perhaps indicated in his advice to Mrs Wheeler who played the part in the Manchester production in 1908, namely, that she should 'discontinue all stage business' during the speech.

The plight of the other women whom we hear of but do not see, is little better. Mrs Simmonds is obviously condemned to years of childbirth; Miss Higgs ended her days in the canal after having lost her modest inheritance; the Pratt girls were denied any kind of education at Miss Thursby's School; Stella's 'plain' German governess 'never came down to dinner'; and Mrs Barnett was evicted from her cottage when her husband died because Sir John Faringford saw its potential as a pigsty. Hankin succeeds, in the same way as Barker, in creating a society as a setting for the particular action of the play, through the mention of a host of outside characters who are made real for the audience, and the image of Chedleigh, though clearly drawn, is hardly pleasant.

Hankin additionally makes use of the parable in order to expound his theories on the deterministic nature of human character. One of the play's most interesting and innovative features is Hankin's investigation into the psychological make-up of society's 'winners' and 'losers'. Eustace has had every advantage, a comfortable and stable family home, a Public School education (denied to the successful Henry), good looks, brains and a pleasant disposition. He is certainly a more attractive personality than Henry, and he sees that although he is strongly attracted to Stella, he could never make her a 'good' husband, and so relinquishes her to his brother whose only motivation is self-interest. He has also had, as his father points out, many chances to redeem himself. Yet he is a failure, 'a thorough detrimental', as Lady Faringford puts it. The fault, he maintains, lies in the character he was born with, harking back, in fact, to the epigraph Hankin uses in the title-page, 'Character is Fate'.

> I'm good for nothing, as you say, I've no push, no initiative, no staying power. I shall never be anything but a failure . . . The real tragedy is what one is. Because one can't escape from that. It's always there, the bundle of passions, weaknesses, stupidities, that one calls character, waiting to trip one up.

Eustace protests that he does not enjoy being a Prodigal. He wishes for success, but some unexplained quality in his psychological make-up marks him out for a 'loser'. Ironically, he implies that this fault lies with his parents for having failed to supply him with the 'genes' necessary to success. Stella Faringford is a 'loser' too, the reason, perhaps, that she is more strongly attracted to Eustace than to Henry. She would like to play the piano, but is quite incapable of following Henry's advice to 'persevere'. 'I suppose I'm lazy. But that's like me. I want to do things. I see I *ought* to do them. But somehow they don't get done'. Such ineffectual excuses are incomprehensible to Henry ('If I want anything, I take the necessary steps to get it.'). He, as Eustace points out, will be a 'winner' anywhere, not as a result of having more brains or more imagination, but because he was born with the requisite strength of character to succeed.

The question to arise is, what ought society to do with its 'losers'? How should it deal with them? The whole concept of Christian charity and forgiveness, as illustrated in the parable, is undercut by a searingly ironic speech by Eustace. In response to Mr Jackson's outraged sense of justice that the 'good' son, Henry, is not paid for his impressive efforts, yet the Prodigal demands, and wins, money to conceal his fecklessness, Eustace eloquently shows his contempt for his father's philosophy:

> It is unreasonable, isn't it? But we live in a humanitarian age. We coddle the sick and we keep alive the imbecile. We shall soon come to pensioning the idle and the dissolute. You're only a little in advance of the times. England is covered with hospitals for the incurably diseased and asylums for the incurably mad. If a tenth of the money were spent on putting such people out of the world, and the rest were used in preventing healthy people from falling sick, and the sane people from starving – we should be a wholesomer nation.

In the same sarcastic vein, Eustace uses the tenets of Darwinism to explain to Stella that according to contemporary social philosophy, there must be good cottages for the strong and poor cottages for the weak. In the materially-orientated world of the Jacksons, only the strong should survive, but it is recognised that from time to time it is necessary to 'pay off' the weak, by public subscriptions, or by annual allowances to keep them out of sight and out of mind.

Hankin chose the parable of the Prodigal to demonstrate that contemporary society had reversed the ethical code expressed in the biblical story. In addition, he reacted in his treatment of the theme against the comfortable sentimentality of the commercial theatre. The fashionable dramatist, Hall Caine, had just enjoyed considerable success with his piece *The Prodigal*, performed at Drury Lane (with real sheep) in 1905. Hankin, as he had shown in *Dramatic Sequels*, was a master of pastiche, and although his play is not a 'send-up' of Caine's, his avoidance of sentiment and his social criticism show how far he was in advance of contemporary theatre practice. *The Return of the Prodigal* was in this respect a typical Court play.

The reviews of the six matinées at the Court, from 26 September to 13 October 1905, were, in general, favourable, although there was a feeling that the high standard of the Court acting contributed in no small measure to the success of the play. Hankin fully acknowledged the contribution of Barker and his company. The piece was put into the evening bill in April 1907, but ran for only two weeks, instead of the four originally intended. Whether its lack of success was because it did not contain the basic elements of popular entertainment (this was Shaw's view) or whether it was too 'tame' for the Court audience is hard to say. It was subsequently revived by Manchester Repertory Theatre in 1908, 1909 and 1910, by the Glasgow Repertory Theatre in 1911 and by Liverpool Rep. in 1912. It became a regular part of Birmingham's repertory and was performed there on ten occasions between 1911 and 1950. John Gielgud led a strong cast at the Globe Theatre in 1948, but the production achieved little acclaim. It is, like most of Hankin's work, 'uncomfortable'. Much might be, and is, said on both sides, and the audience is left uncertain as to where its sympathies should lie. This is even more true of the next two pieces, *The Charity that began at Home* and *The Cassilis Engagement*.

The Charity that began at Home
This piece, subtitled 'A Comedy for Philanthropists', tells the story of Lady Denison and her daughter, Margery, who, under the influence of Basil Hylton, a lay preacher, an amateur social worker and leader of the Church of Humanity, invite to their home a group of social 'failures' to whom no other hostess will give house room. As Lady Denison puts it, '*False* hospitality is inviting people because

you like them. *True* hospitality is inviting them because they'd like to be asked.' The guests are General Bonsor, a retired officer from the Indian Army and a celebrated bore, Mr Firket who has failed in the City and is now selling (or rather 'pushing') a variety of products on commission, Mrs Horrocks, who is vulgar and quarrelsome, Miss Triggs, a governess with a special interest in teaching German, who is rude, and Hugh Verreker, who at first sight gives the impression of being a young man of wit and charm, but who, it emerges, has had to resign from the Army as a result of his fraudulent appropriation of mess funds. The only person who is present in her own right and not because she is a 'lame duck' is Lady Denison's outspoken sister-in-law, Mrs Eversleigh, who takes a poor view of her fellow guests and of her relations' idiosyncracy.

Not only in her choice of house-guests, but also in her appointment of servants, Lady Denison practices philan-thropic idealism. The electricity supply is spasmodic be-cause the dynamo is run by an alcoholic ex-footman whom no-one else will employ. The butler, Soames, has been appointed out of charity, because he has no character references and a reputation for petty larceny. He antago-nises William, Lady Denison's long-serving and faithful footman, and seduces her excellent maid. The cook gives notice as a protest against the irregularities of the house-hold which is sadly depleted by the end of the play. As Mrs Eversleigh acidly remarks to her sister, this state of affairs is 'the logical outcome of your theories, when applied to domestic service'.

The sacrifices Lady Denison has to make for her principles extend far beyond the crocheting of violently coloured blankets for the partially sighted and her attempt to learn German to please the brusque Miss Trigg. Hugh Verreker proposes marriage to Margery and is accepted.

After all, Hylton had implied that Hugh could be 'saved' if he 'fell into the right hands', and Margery is a philanthropist to the core. General Bonsor reveals the truth about Hugh's malpractice in the army, and in retaliation, Hugh tells the guests about the unflattering grounds for their invitations. Highly insulted, all the objects of Denison charity depart, except for Hugh, but he, with great regret, gives up the idea of marrying Margery, recognising that her selflessness would be incompatible with his hedonistic philosophy. As he says to her, 'You look on life as a moral discipline. I look on it as a means to enjoyment.' He recommends that she marry Basil Hylton, a 'good' man who loves her. Apparently, by (yet again) eschewing the happy ending of a marriage, Hankin denied himself a West End production. George Alexander told him that he had spoiled the play as a business proposition by not giving it a conventional conclusion.

Apart from the ill-assorted guests and the troubled domestic staff, the characters represent three different philosophies. Basil Hylton and his disciples, Margery and Lady Denison, profess a fervent idealism, and admire 'the saints and martyrs' that have laid down their lives for great causes. They believe in the fundamental, if latent, goodness of human nature that needs only patience, kindness and love to bring it to the surface. Although Lady Denison does show signs of strain in her efforts towards perfection, Margery embraces the creed with energy and total commitment. Basil Hylton is possessed with 'a divine madness'. His philosophy is summed up in his plea for the retention of the services of the troublesome Soames, 'Wicked people are only weak people, Lady Denison. If they were strong they would resist temptation. But they are weak, and they yield to it.' Hugh Verreker is a Shavian in his philosphical distrust of idealism. Ideals are for 'other people', and in an echo from *The Quintessence of Ibsenism*, he asserts, 'If people would only give up bothering about ideals and face facts, what a much happier world this would be for all of us.' The moral institutions of society, such as love and religious faith, he sees as two of 'the seven deadly virtues', an echo of Shaw's Don Juan in *Man and Superman*, 'Hell is the home of honor, duty, justice and the rest of the seven deadly virtues. All the wickedness on earth is done in their name.' Like the deterministic Eustace in *The Return of the Prodigal* whom he, in many respects, resembles, Hugh believes that one's character is formed at birth, 'Some people are born self-denying just as other people are born self-indulgent.' Since Margery belongs clearly to the former category and he to the latter, although he loves her, he recognises that the marriage is doomed to failure. Marriages built on love rather than compatibility will founder, and as he says, he and Margery 'have not got an idea or a taste in common'. He, therefore, asks to be released from his engagement, and so performs the most 'noble' act in his life: 'For the first, and I hope the last, time in my life I've done an unselfish act.' Ironically, Margery has succeeded in converting Hugh, although she thinks that she has failed. The man with no prospects relinquishes the heiress whom he loves, because he is convinced that the marriage would make her unhappy. Hugh, of course, 'would have been all right'.

Hugh practises and preaches common-sense, the quality which warned him against marriage with Margery, and which leads him to regard as ridiculous the current organisation of charitable institutions, exemplified by the Orphanage, since it is clear that all the effort and postage expended on supporting individual orphans, might well have endowed another orphanage. This common sense is shared with the formidable Mrs Eversleigh. But whereas

Hugh is iconoclastic in his attitude both to philanthropy and to received social dogma, Mrs Eversleigh is a stout upholder of society's dictates. If indeed Basil Hylton is so outstandingly eligible, she can regard Lady Denison's eccentric behaviour as the legitimate efforts of a 'good' mother to secure a 'good' marriage for her daughter. But, as philanthropy is seen to lead to increasing absurdity and discomfort, she speaks out, 'It's trying to regulate one's life by a theory instead of by the light of common sense.' Her attitude to Margery's proposed marriage displays her strict adherence to social convention. A man of Verreker's background ought not to have proposed marriage to the daughter of his hostess. Margery, in accepting such an unsuitable proposal, first on humanitarian grounds, and then admitting that she loves Hugh, 'has no moral sense whatever' – an obvious equating of morality with conventional behaviour.

Yet Mrs Eversleigh is not unattractive in her down-to-earth pragmatism, just as Lady Denison is appealing in her frayed philanthropy. This is a much 'pleasanter' play than *The Return of the Prodigal*, for although, as William Phillips points out, Hankin does not in the end 'reform' his philanthropists in the manner of Shaw in *Major Barbara*, (another play which demonstrates the folly and political ineffectiveness of private charity), the social criticism is less vicious and the social comedy more astute.

It is in this play, more than in Hankin's earlier work, that St John Ervine's comment that Hankin's stage directions have the effect of the Chorus in Greek tragedy is apposite. When the faithful footman, William, and the recalcitrant Soames are serving tea, the Stage Direction reads, '*A certain hostility is just visible between them, but very discreetly shown.*' When General Bonsor discovers that he has been invited because he is such a bore that no-one else will ask him to visit, the Stage Direction suddenly reveals the pitiable character behind the garrulous old soldier: '*There is a pause while we realise that one of the most tragic things in life is to be a bore – and to know it.*' Both examples are useful to actors in giving guidelines to performance.

The play was staged at the Court in October/November 1906 for eight matinées. Although William Archer, writing in *The Tribune* (24 October 1906) thought it Hankin's best play to date (a view shared by Granville Barker) other critics found the plot 'slight', and Grein in *The Sunday Times* (28 October 1906) compared it unfavourably with the plays of Barker and with Galsworthy's *The Silver Box*, while the critic of the *Saturday Review* (27 October 1906) thought it a poor and pretentious imitation of Wilde and Shaw, without the wit of either. Desmond MacCarthy saw the inconclusive ending as its deficiency. 'At the close of the play you are left in doubt as to which of the characters are meant to be in the right and which in the wrong.' The point is that no one is all right nor all wrong, and one of the constraints of the propagandist leaning of many of the Court plays may have been that critics and audiences came to expect a clear line, a firm point of view. *Charity* followed *The Silver Box* in the matinée series, and while it was playing, *Man and Superman* was in the evening bill. It is hardly surprising that Hankin's piece was felt to be slight by comparison.

Although the pace of the production (by Granville Barker) was criticised as being too slow, the acting in general found favour, particularly Dennis Eadie as General Bonsor ('an exaggerated and obsolete type' according to the *Saturday Review*), Ben Webster as Verreker, and Florence Haydon as Lady Denison.

Like *The Return of the Prodigal*, the play was popular with the provincial repertory theatres. It was revived in

Manchester in 1908 and 1913, at Liverpool in 1913, and had three performances at Birmingham in 1915, 1916 and 1917. Since then it has remained without a professional production in Britain and has been out of print since 1914.

The Cassilis Engagement

It is in this play that Hankin states most explicitly his antipathy to the romantic marriage. Geoffrey Cassilis, a young man of the landed gentry, whose godmother and aunt are titled ladies, meets and falls in love with a young woman from London, called Ethel Borridge. Her sister, we learn, is a prostitute; her mother lived for years with her father before enticing him into matrimony. The aristocratic society around Deynham, the Cassilis country seat, is shocked by the news of the proposed misalliance, and surprised at the apparently permissive attitude of Geoffrey's mother, who, far from forbidding the match, seems to be encouraging it by inviting Ethel and her mother to stay. Mrs Cassilis's tactics prove successful. Ethel is bored to death by the country and breaks off the engagement, leaving Geoffrey free to contract a much more suitable match with his godmother's daughter, Lady Mabel Remenham. He remains devoted to his mother who has been throughout supportive to him and charming to his projected bride and to her vulgar mother. Reason and brains defeat romance, and another marriage 'that would have ended in the Divorce Court, as such marriages always do' is avoided. The motto of the play might well be Hugh Verreker's line in *The Charity that began at Home*, 'Marriage isn't a thing to be romantic about. It lasts too long.'

Hankin, in *Dramatic Sequels*, had already satirised T.W. Robertson's *Caste*, which had advocated that 'love can leap over' class barriers, and that, provided that the woman in question is 'a natural lady', she need have no fears about her ultimate acceptance by her husband's aristocratic relations. The name 'Borridge' has echoes of 'Gerridge' in the earlier play, a name which, as the Marquise de St Maur remarks, one breaks one's teeth on. In this 'Sequel', Hankin comically demonstrated that in marrying one is not only taking a partner for life, but acquiring a whole set of new relations, who cannot be dismissed as easily as Robertson proposed in *Caste*. Ethel's boarding school education may have given her a superficial polish, but Geoffrey would never be free of the vulgar Mrs Borridge, with her brightly coloured blouses, her dropped aitches and her frankly money-grubbing aspirations. As Major Warrington remarks to him, 'You'll never be able to keep them apart.'

In pursuing with faultless logic the line that marriage shoud be built on compatibility of tastes and interests, rather than on komanmic love, Hankin might well be considered a reactionary in making explicit the view that the gulf between the aristocracy and the lower classes is unbridgeable. The elegant, clever and beautiful Mrs Cassilis is greatly to be preferred to the overweight, badly-dressed and boring Mrs Borridge. One of the faults of the piece was thought by contemporary critics to be the characterisation of the latter, although Clare Greet, 'the most inimitable of actresses', who played the part in the first Stage Society production, saved it from total caricature. There is no suggestion, as there undoubtedly would have been if Shaw had treated the same theme, that it was very easy for Mrs Cassilis to be so civilised and so clever, whereas it had taken a considerable amount of grit and will-power by Mrs Borridge and Ethel to get themselves into a position to be invited to Deynham at all.

Although Ethel is described by her future husband as 'not quite a lady', in the stage directions as 'pretty but second-rate', and in the prefatory essay as 'a young woman with neither birth, nor amiability nor good manners', a great deal exists in the text that would allow an actress to counter this view. In the first place, Ethel shows a sympathy for her fellow creatures that is sadly lacking in most of the inhabitants of Deynham. She has sympathy with her 'fallen' sister, and although she fully appreciates her mother's social *gaffes*, she retains a fondness for her. She did, after all, reject Lord Buckfastleigh's offer to accompany him to Paris in spite of the substantial reward of £5,000 which he proposed to give her for her services, and her wistful recollection of Johnny Travers, who, although only an auctioneer's clerk, made her laugh, is rather touching. Although she has had a reasonable education she recognises with the determinism prevalent in many of Hankin's characters that, 'It can't alter how we're made, can it?' But she is not stupid, certainly not in matters of human relations, and she sees clearly that Lady Marchmont is taking a perverse pleasure in egging her mother on to commit more and more social blunders. It is significant that it is she, not Geoffrey, who has the wit to break off the engagement, recognising fully Mrs Cassilis's point about incompatibility. 'I don't think we're suited to each other.' She also realises that marriage is not about romance, and that 'love' is not necessarily 'for ever'. In the first act she remarks that, had her engagement been terminated:

I'm not the sort to go moping around for long. I should have been awfully down for a bit, and missed you every day. But by-and-by I should have cheered up and married someone else.

She might well have proved to be an ally for Mrs Cassilis in the debate between reason and sentiment, had the author not stacked the cards against her.

The incident of the two after-dinner songs in Act III also reveals the strain of independence in Ethel's character. After Mabel's song, sung in German 'in a small but sweet voice', Ethel's music-hall piece is a clear act of defiance, as Warrington remarks, 'magnificent, but it was scarcely tactics'. Ethel's outburst of self-justification is one of her most impressive moments in the play.

> Here they have been despising me all evening for nothing, and when that detestable girl with a voice like a white mouse sang her German jargon, praising her sky-high, I said I'd show them what singing means! And I did!

She did indeed. During Mabel's song, *'the behaviour of the guests affords a striking illustration of the English attitude towards music after dinner'*, that is, mild boredom and indifference concealed by apparent close attention. Ethel's song, however, galvanises the Deynham society into some kind of activity, even if it is only outrage at her 'bad taste'. Judged from the point of view of 'effect on one's audience', there is no doubt which performer had more success. The fact that the part of Ethel was played in the Stage Society production by Maudi Darrell, a music-hall artiste, whose first 'straight' role this was, must have strengthened the power of the scene.

It is Geoffrey's criticism of the singing incident that causes Ethel to rebel. She senses, rightly, a denial of her individuality, a will to change her, which she instantly rejects. 'I shall do exactly what I please', a primitive but forceful denial of the threatened subordination. The 'quarrel' gives her the courage to reject Geoffrey and Deynham in the final act, which she does without any vulgar 'breach of promise' suit.

> I don't want your carriages and pair. Give me a penny omnibus. It *is* vulgar, isn't it? But *I'm* vulgar. And I'm not ashamed of it.

If what Ethel renounces is the daily ride round the policies, the walk to Milverton Hill, the occasional trip to the strawberry patch, and the company of the unpleasant Lady Remenham and the ineffectual vicar, it is no great loss to her. Life at Deynham is presented as fairly idle and useless. Hankin, in the Preface, provides his own dramatic sequel, that she will marry Lord Buckfastleigh and worry him into his grave in six months. If one may presume to provide Hankin with an alternative 'sequel', one would guess that she would marry Johnny Travers and obtain for him a peerage for services to the preservation of the National Heritage.

Ethel's antagonist, however, is not the weak and romantic Geoffrey but his much more intelligent and pragmatic mother, Mrs Cassilis. She is the spokeswoman for marriage based on compatibility to tastes and interests, and while she is undeniably right in her assessment that Ethel and Geoffrey will never make a good match, one cannot help but feel that the real obstacle is Geoffrey's conventionality and not Ethel's vulgar background. The character was berated as being 'a wicked soulless woman' by the dramatic critics, no doubt because she denies the possibility of romantic love. As part of her plot to sabotage the engagement, she pretends to admire its 'romantic' nature. 'Yes, Geoffrey has got engaged to a girl in London. Isn't it *romantic* of him?' The fact that he met her in an accident on

an omnibus is 'romantic' too. It is this 'romance' that must
be countered.

> There's fascination about a runaway match. It has
> romance. Whereas there's no romance about an ordin-
> ary wedding. It's only dull and rather vulgar.

Neither Lady Remenham nor Lady Marchmont, both of
whom one presumes had 'ordinary weddings', seem particularly close to their husbands. The absence of one partner
from the other seems to be a positive blessing. But Mrs
Cassilis, according to Hankin 'neither an idiot nor a
sentimentalist', is intent on killing her future daughter-in-
law with kindness in order to prevent a tragic mistake by
her son. Her invitations to Lady Mabel, with whom
Geoffrey clearly has a great deal in common, and to Major
Warrington whose purpose is to remind Ethel of the
exciting London 'high-life', are part of the masterplan. So
clever is her plan, so hypocritical her behaviour, that even
her sister, Lady Marchmont, comes to pity Ethel. Her
conviction in the rightness of her course of action and in her
capacity for successfully bringing it to fruition – 'I've brains
and she hasn't. And brains always tell in the end' – is
unshakeable. Her success means that she keeps Geoffrey's
love for her intact, while destroying his 'romantic' attach-
ment to Ethel. There is not a hint of criticism of the
conventional parent/child relationship, as there is in Ibsen.
The bond between mother and son remains unquestioned.
Evelyn Weedon, the actress who played Mrs Cassilis,
stressed the aspect of mother-love rather than that of the
rational woman.

Once again, Hankin leaves the reader or the spectator in
an ambivalent frame of mind: Mrs Cassilis is right, for the
wrong reasons; Geoffrey is wrong, for the right reasons. It

is difficult to say whether the implied criticism of the life style of the upper-middle-class is intentional or not, or whether the wit is gratuitous or pointed. There is no doubt that the piece is open to several interpretations.

Contemporary critics were not, on the whole, impressed. The play was seen as amusing, but 'thin'. J.T. Grein writing in *The Sunday Times* (17 February 1907) went so far as to berate the Stage Society for accepting such a *vieux jeu* piece at all. It was seen as 'clever comedy of upper-class life' by critic of *The Era* (16 February 1907), as 'a criticism of life written by an agreeable trifler' by H.H. Fyfe in *The World* (19 February 1907). The lack of sentiment and melodramatic tendencies were appreciated (*The Star*, 12 February 1907) but generally the feeling was that *The Cassilis Engagement* was little more than a pleasant light comedy.

After the performance by the Stage Society at the Imperial Theatre on 10 February 1907, the play was not presented again in London by a professional company. It was, however, like Hankin's other work, popular in the provincial repertory theatres, playing twice in Glasgow (1910, 1911), three times in Liverpool (1911 [on tour], 1912, 1915) and many times in Birmingham between 1913 and 1949.

The Last of the De Mullins

In this, his last complete full-length play, Hankin consolidates and reworks themes which he used in his earlier works. As in *The Return of the Prodigal*, a recalcitrant member of a respectable middle-class family comes back to expose the deficiencies of the stay-at-homes, but whereas Eustace returns as a failure, Janet De Mullin, in her new persona, the widow, Mrs Seagrave, is a financial and personal success. The Jacksons, social *parvenus* though they might be, are in the ascendancy: the ancient house of De Mullin is in decline.

The family of the De Mullins have lived in the village of Brendon since the time of King Stephen, and have occupied their present home for four hundred years. The illness of the head of the family, Hugo De Mullin, prompts his wife, Jane, to contact their elder daughter, Janet, who left home some eight years previously when she became pregnant by an unknown man. Janet returns to the family seat with her son, Johnny, to face her father and mother, her sister, Hester, a religious and plain woman who is attracted to the local curate, Mr Brown, and her sharp-tongued aunt, Mrs Clouston. In the course of her visit, she meets the father of her child, Monty Bulstead, who has just become engaged to one of the local gentry. The reunion convinces her that she was right not to marry such an 'uninteresting' man, and despite her father's invitation (indeed his command) to stay in Brendon, she leaves to return to her prosperous hat-shop in London. She has no wish for her son to become a De Mullin nor to hinder her sister's marriage prospects because of her own unconventional life-style, and with an impassioned speech on the importance of a woman's independence and her fulfilment in the bearing and rearing of children, either within or without matrimony, she exits, leaving the 'ghosts' of the De Mullin household to their ancestral pride and inherent decay.

The Mill from which they took their name is no longer in use; their land has dwindled; their heath is failing. Far from gaining strength and succour from their roots in Brendon, they have become so debilitated that it is only through the presence of Janet, the *deracinée* daughter, and her son that Hugo seems able to regain his health. Simultaneously, being in Brendon sucks away Janet's vitality so that she becomes irritable and petty. Her independent rationality can only exist away from the family home.

Hugo De Mullin at the beginning of the play sees himself in the title role – he calls himself 'the last of the De Mullins' – but later confers the title on Johnny. Janet, however, refuses to accept the description of her son. She does not want him to be a De Mullin, deliberately choosing for him a Christian name that is not in the family tradition, because to her to be one implies idleness, uselessness, constraint, and sickness. The corrupt will die, because the last of the line who regards it as his primary duty 'to be healthy and happy' will bear neither the name nor the burden that accompanies it.

In this play, Hankin repeats the pattern of characters which he has used throughout his work, the 'heavy' father (Mr Jackson and Mr De Mullin), the good-hearted but simple-minded mother (Mrs Jackson, Lady Denison, Mrs De Mullin), the other older woman of sharp tongue and socially conventional morality (Lady Faringford, Mrs Eversleigh, Lady Remenham and Mrs Clouston), and the 'rebel' of the younger generation (Eustace, Hugh Verreker, Ethel Borridge and Major Warrington, and Janet). The young people who accept almost without question the opinions and *mores* of their elders (Henry and Violet Jackson, Mabel Remenham, and Hester De Mullin) are seen partly as victims and partly as unthinking pawns in a corrupt social game.

Hankin's most significant step forward in *The Last of the De Mullins* is seen in his full-blooded entry into the women's rights debate that he touched on in Violet's speech in *The Return of the Prodigal*. Janet De Mullin is without question 'a new woman' in the tradition of Barker and Shaw. Like Barker's Ann Leete, she will save a decadent House by leaving it; like Marion Yates, she will bring up her child without its father whom she does not care for; like Shaw's Eliza Doolittle, she will turn to honest trade rather than accept an unsatisfactory marriage. She rejects out of hand the notion of a woman as a dependent and an obedient servant. When her father attempts to assert paternal authority, she replies in anger.

> Obedience! Obedience! I owe no one obedience. I am of full age and can order my life as I please. Is a women never to be considered old enough to manage her own affairs? Is she to go down to her grave everlastingly under tutelage? Is she always to be obeying a father when she's not obeying a husband? Well, I for one will not submit to such nonsense. I'm sick of this everlasting obedience.

Her outspoken views are a world apart from those of her family who believe that, 'The only independence that is possible or desirable for a woman is that she shall be dependent upon her husband or, if she is unmarried, on her nearest male relative.'

Hankin, like Shaw and like Barker, links the whole concept of 'new womanhood' with the bearing and upbringing of a child, without necessarily demanding, or indeed desiring, the support of the child's father. Janet De Mullin's last speech, urging women towards procreation is a clear expression of the 'new dramatist's' creed for the 'new woman'.

> These poor women who go through life listless and dull, who have never felt the joys and pains a mother feels, how they would envy me if they knew. If they knew! To know that a child is part of you. That you have faced sickness and pain and death itself for it. That it is yours

and nothing can take it from you because no one understands it as you do. To feel its soft breath on your cheek, to soothe it when it is fretful and still it when it cries, that is motherhood and that is glorious!

Hankin barely allows the child's father, Monty Bulstead, the 'father's heart' that Shaw gave to John Tanner and Barker gave to Henry Trebell. He is fond of the child, kisses him three times, but is clearly relieved that Janet has no desire to affirm his paternity and upset his proposed marriage to the eligible and pretty Bertha Aldenham.

Janet finds maternity so satisfying that she even urges her religious sister, Hester to marry the first curate who comes along so that she too can, in respectability, reproduce. Hester, who has hated Janet throughout the play is sufficiently reconciled to embrace her on parting. There is no sense that it is a Shavian 'Life Force' that inspires her words, but the doctrine is clearly stated that a free woman's fulfilment, (however successful and enterprising in business she might be) lies in procreation. Johnny's health and fearlessness testify to the success of Janet's brand of motherhood.

Hankin also demonstrates the conventional prejudices that constrained a woman's progress to self-realisation. Janet is lucky because she had a modest inheritance from an aunt, but according to Mrs Clouston's philosophy, she should not have been allowed to administer it herself (despite the fact that by shrewd investment she has increased her legacy by 25%). The 'respectable' occupations of teacher or governess were so badly paid that she could not have hoped to support herself and her offspring on such a salary. Even her entry into trade has had to be founded on a lie, the sea-widow story of the appropriately named Mrs Seagrave. Respectable women at home like

Hester are restricted by their families' pretensions in seeking a husband; spinsters, like Miss Deane expend their maternity on 'poultry', as Janet cruelly describes the lady's pet cockatoo; Mrs De Mullin is a 'crushed' and servile wife. Janet is, at her entrance, before the vampire-like society of Deynham tries to suck her blood, wealthy, positive, confident – and a mother.

It was the fact that the fallen woman was shown to be successful and happy that disturbed even the avant-garde audience of the Stage Society which presented the play in December 1908. 'Bad' women, however much sympathy was elicited for their cause by pretty costumes and fine acting performances, had to be seen as 'repentant' (if not as dead) at the end of the play. So, Hankin, who with some justification had been criticised as 'cynical', 'negative', and for a 'new dramatist' insufficiently 'propagandist' had written a 'thesis' play. *The Star* (8 December 1908) complained that the propagandist purpose predominated, rendering the piece 'nerveless and bloodless'. *The World* (8 December 1908) appreciated Hankin's attack on 'the good old family' but criticised the slow pace of W. Graham Browne's production. Shaw, too, felt the piece had been badly directed. The acting, on the other hand, particularly Lillah McCarthy's performance as Janet, which persuaded the critic of *The World* that 'she was a woman and not a bundle of feminist philosophies' was highly praised, understandably, since the cast was made up of a large number of former Court actors. Yet Shaw regretted the tendency to stereotype roles, particularly the rendering of Monty Bulstead as 'the vulgar sentimental hero of a thousand bad plays'. The scene between Monty and Janet he thought was 'the best thing Hankin has yet done' and the Stage Society's production failed to do it justice.

Shaw is wise in his assessment. The characterisation is

not sacrificed to the problem; a positive, if difficult, solution is proferred, and the play presents an optimism not usually present in Hankin's works. This play 'without a Preface' is the most Shavian of all.

4
John Masefield

John Masefield was born at Ledbury in Herefordshire in 1878. Orphaned at an early age, he was brought up by his aunt and uncle until he was old enough to be sent to the King's School, Warwick. After he had attempted several escapes from an environment that he clearly found uncongenial, it was decided that he should finish his education aboard the merchant service training ship, HMS Conway. From 1891–95, he was a sailor, but his fascination with New York prompted him to leave his ship, and for the next two years he took several menial jobs, such as bartender and carpet factory worker, in the United States. Shortly after his return to England in 1897, he became involved with W.B. Yeats and J.M. Synge, and published his first book of poetry *Sea Water Ballads* in 1902. His devotion to the countryside of his childhood and his admiration for the Irish school of drama are both evident in his dramatic writing particularly in his best play *The Tragedy of Nan*, which is dedicated to Yeats.

His introduction to the Court Theatre reads like a theatrical romance. Barker asked Theodore Stier, the company's musical director, to find sea chanties for the second act of Shaw's *Captain Brassbound's Conversion*, which was presented at the Court in April 1906. A boy came into Barker's office professing to be adept at making up sea songs. Barker asked Stier to see him.

> And sure enough at the appointed time on the following
> day a slim, poorly dresssed, and very shy young seaman
> insinuated himself through the door of my sanctum. 'Mr
> Barker told me to come and whistle to you,' he said
> diffidently, twirling his cap in his hands. 'That's all
> right,' I said. 'Sit down and let me hear those sea
> chanties I've heard so much about.' So, very stiff and
> upright in a chair, the young sailor went through the
> tunes that in his spare time he had composed in the
> forecastle of a wooden sailing ship. When he got up to
> go, obviously relieved that his ordeal was at an end, I
> asked him his name. 'John Masefield,' he said.'

Masefield became fascinated by the art of the theatre.
Attracted by Barker, Galsworthy and Yeats he felt that the
most stimulating literary activity of the time was in drama,
and in drama at the Court Theatre in particular. His first
play, *The Campden Wonder*, was presented at the Court in
a series of experimental matinées in January/February
1907. Granville Barker and Lillah McCarthy were closely
involved in the production of *The Tragedy of Nan* by the
Pioneer Players in 1908 and in Masefield's adaptation of
The Witch by Wiens Jensson, first produced by the Glasgow
Repertory Theatre in 1911. He continued to write dramatic
pieces until 1933, although latterly not for performance in
the professional theatre, but for private presentation in his
own theatre at his home in Berkshire. His other plays
include *The Tragedy of Pompey the Great* (1910), *Philip the
King* (1914), *The Faithful* (1915), *Good Friday* (1916), *A
King's Daughter* (1923), *Tristan and Isolde* (1927), *The
Coming of Christ* (1928) and *End and Beginning* (1933).
Masefield is more celebrated as a poet than as a dramatist

and in 1930 he was appointed Poet Laureate by King George V. He died in 1967, and his ashes were interred in Poet's Corner in Westminster Abbey.

Masefield is in several respects an atypical 'new dramatist'. In the first place, the settings of his first two pieces are rural and lower-class. With the exception of a few scenes in Galsworthy's plays, the 'new dramatists' deal exclusively with middle-class society that formed the bulk of the Court audiences. Masefield shows himself to be more at home among his farmworkers, and reveals not only a real feeling for the rural environment, but a sensitivity towards the peasantry that is neither patronising nor sentimental. He is closer to Synge and to Yeats than to Barker and Galsworthy in his attempt to create a folk-drama for the English theatre, seen clearly in the shift in setting from the drawing room to the farm kitchen. The shift 'below stairs' is not motivated by any desire to dramatise or to make explicit the poverty of the rural workers. Physical hardship is not presented as a major factor in either play, and there is no resentment expressed towards those more fortunate, indeed they are barely mentioned. There is some criticism of the fatuity of the Church and of the insensitivity of the Law, but no suggestion that these institutions would act any differently towards the more prosperous members of the community. Masefield is even less propagandist than the writers of nineteenth-century melodrama in this respect.

Secondly, in Masefield's plays, debate or philosophising, beloved of the 'new dramatists', is replaced by incident and action. There are three hangings in *The Campden Wonder*, and a murder (on stage) as well as a suicide (off stage) in *The Tragedy of Nan*. The violence of characters' actions is the necessary corollary of the violence of emotion which they express. Masefield felt that contemporary drama was lacking in two things, what he called 'the power of

exultation' and 'a poetic impulse'. 'The power of exultation' could he believed, only be expressed, by delighted
brooding on excessive terrible things – hence the strong
emotions of love and hate and vengeance that motivate his
characters. He endorsed William Archer's view of drama as
'conflict', but the conflict is primitive and elemental,
between the forces of good and evil, rather than between
man and man or man and society. 'Tragedy is at its best a
vision of the heart of life. The heart of life can only be laid
bare in the agony and exultation of dreadful acts.'
Although a bare description of the plot might well lead one
to think that Masefield is writing melodrama, the 'excess' of
the action is always justified by the powerful feelings from
which it grows.

Although both *The Campden Wonder* and *The Tragedy
of Nan* are written in prose, in moments of stress the
characters' language becomes highly charged and figurative. If they are inarticulate in terms of rhetoric and
self-analysis, their language is not always naturalistic in the
sense that it is 'the real language of men'. This has laid
Masefield open to the accusation that he is over-literary, in
that the imagery is too carefully contrived to be happily
acceptable in the mouths of his rustics. But his use of
language fits perfectly with his theory of drama, and even
the short and simple sentences demand from the actors an
emotional heat and intensity in delivery. The settings may
be ordinary and commonplace, but the leading characters
are so exceptional as to be seen as the symbols or
mouthpieces of vice or virtue, like those in a morality play.

Masefield took his inspiration from the Irish school of
'new dramatists' such as Yeats or Synge, rather than from
the English, but he shared with both sets of reformers the
belief that the theatre needed to be more than mere
entertainment, a thoughtless diversion for the comfortable

middle-classes. He continued to feel this way even after his professional associations with the theatre had ceased. It is unfortunate that after *The Tragedy of Nan* he chose to turn to classical or religious subjects and ultimately to eschew the professional theatre, for in his first two plays there is evidence of a power and an originality of style that could have benefited the English theatre in the later part of the century.

The Campden Wonder

The Campden Wonder tells the story of Joan Perry and her two sons, John and Dick. Dick is a sober, hard-working young man, devoted to his wife and his family, but John is an idle drunkard. Envious of the high regard which Richard enjoys in the community and more specifically of his increased wage of twelve shillings a week, John hatches a vicious plot. When the brothers' employer, Mr Harrison, disappears, John claims that he has been murdered for his gold by the entire Perry family. This rather unlikely story is believed by the Parson and by the Court, and the whole family is hanged. Minutes after the miscarriage of justice, Mrs Harrison, who has never believed in the Perrys' guilt, enters to announce that her husband has returned, apparently having been out on a drunken binge. Horrified by the terrible mistake, Mrs Harrison and the Parson join hands in tearful prayers. Masefield added a short piece, entitled *Mrs Harrison*, which was not performed. We learn that Harrison was party to John Perry's scheme. He was given £300 to 'disappear', and to delay his return until after the Perry family had been hanged. Mrs Harrison, overcome by the knowledge that she has been living with a person who was an accessory to murder, commits suicide by taking poison.

179

Both the play and its unperformed sequel are riddled with improbabilities. Dick's friendship with the Parson has been described scathingly by John early in the first scene. It is highly unlikely that the clergyman would take the word of a known reprobate against that of his upstanding friend on the flimsy evidence of Dick having a piece of twine in his pocket that John asserts is the murder weapon. The Parson is also swayed by the fact that when Dick is called upon to swear his innocence on the Bible he almost faints and is afflicted with a nose bleed. 'His nose is bleeding. It is the hand of God. God has spoken, Tom.' It is unclear in the sequel who bribed Harrison to stay away. Harrison says the money came from the 'Lord', perhaps simply implying that it appeared to come as a gift from Heaven. Where would the impecunious John get £300, unless he stole it? In addition, it is hard to believe that Mrs Harrison, who has not been presented at all as a stupid woman, and who in fact was the person who resolutely refused to believe John's story, would mistake the day of the Perry's hanging and so arrive too late to save them. It is possible that Masefield intended to use the coincidence of Dick's nose bleed at the moment of swearing on the Bible, and Mrs Harrison's mistake about the time of the hanging to demonstrate the conflict of human beings against Fate, rather in the manner of Thomas Hardy with whom he is often compared. He certainly believed that such conflict was the essence of drama. Desmond MacCarthy called the play 'a piece of life', but even allowing for the fact that an audience is more credulous than a reader, it is hard to believe that such a far-fetched tale convinced the Court patrons.

The strength of the piece does not lie in its narrative, but rather in the single-minded picture of unremitting evil that it presents. John has no redeeming features: he is pure vice, embodying drunkenness, envy, sloth, vengeance and murder. No adequate motivation is provided for his crime. It is true that his mother may have been over-indulgent because of his marked resemblance to his late father, certainly she accuses herself of this as she faces death. 'I've been a great sinner, and I be punished for it. I set my boy John afore my boy Dick.' It is true that Dick is somewhat self-righteous and censorious in his relations with his brother, and that John resents him. 'You was like the good boy in the Bible, you always was.' This sneer from an irredeemable prodigal who also describes his brother as 'an innocent lamb', might be seen as an attempt to lift the conflict of the brothers from the personal to the elemental. But Masefield uses neither Joan's misplaced leniency nor Dick's smugness as excuses for the vengeful hatred of John's threat, 'I'll bring you low – I'll bring you lower than the lowest.'

In prison, John exults in his evil. He remembers with glee the trial, the Judge in his red gown, the sword before him; he looks forward with anticipation to the hanging and the notoriety that will follow it,

> Us'll have ballads sung – and I shouldn't wonder. Us'll all be in a ballad. 'The bloody Perrys, they was hanged – O, grief!' And there'll be drums, and the sun a-shining – on Broadway Hill and all. And there'll be neighbours. Sure to be. And us'll go in a cart, like high up folk. 'There they go'; neighbours'll say, 'as killed un for ens gold. They was always bad ones, them Perrys, they'll say.

This piece of self-dramatisation in which John sees himself as a folk hero like Dick Turpin or Ned Kelly, is cleverly juxtaposed by Masefield between a touching speech by Dick full of concern for the future of his little daughter, 'Her were saying so pretty – and I shan't see un again...

And her'll want bread to eat, and go to bed crying!' and Joan's lament that she will not be buried in the churchyard with her dead husband. The three speeches are like three prose poems expressing the essential nature of each individual, rather than dialogue designed to show the interaction of characters. Here one can see Masefield pushing towards verse drama.

As far as the language of the play is concerned, the authenticity of the dialect is not important. It *seems* to be authentic, and would sound so. More importantly, its forcefulness provides Masefield at moments of passion with a springboard to a heightened poetic prose style, for example, the simple inversion in 'For his gold we murdered him', and the use of biblical references in which Mrs Harrison expresses her fears about her husband's whereabouts.

> He's been seen with the scarlet woman! He's been sitting on the seven hills, I know it. O dear, O dear, drinking the wine of wrath.

Language is also used to contrast the characters of the Parson and Tom, the constable, in the death cell, the latter speaking in straightforward terms of practical things:

> Mrs Harrison have took Dick's little ones. God save 'ee, Mother. Us knows as you be innocent. And neighbours say it. God bless 'ee Dick. If I don't see ee again.

His words bring more comfort to Dick about his family and to Mrs Perry about her good name, than the Parson's platitudes:

Ah, Mrs Perry! In a few moments you will be before God's Judgement Seat, a trembling bird on God's hand.

MacCarthy calls *The Campden Wonder* 'simply a tragic story', but other critical opinion denied its status as a tragedy, on the grounds that none of the characters is sufficiently admirable. Dick, although a decent and industrious man, does not show any courage in facing the death that Fate, in the shape of his brother, deals him. His reaction is psychologically sound, but it is not heroic. Joan Perry, although she is self-aware enough to recognise the consequences of her sentimental partiality for John, is hardly of the stature to make a tragic heroine. Their loss does not, therefore, promote a truly tragic sense of waste in the audience, however sad it might be in naturalistic terms. Only John, in his Iago-like malevolence, rises above the commonplace. The play's strength lies in the portrayal of a psychopath. In its pathos, it has more in common with melodrama than with tragedy.

It was first performed in a series of eight matinées at the Court Theatre in January/February 1907. It was not a success, partly because of a mistaken managerial decision to put it on a double bill with Cyril Harcourt's very light comedy, *The Reformer*. The style of the two pieces was quite incompatible, and because of Cyril Harcourt's demanding behaviour during rehearsals, not enough attention was given to Masefield's piece. The performances, with the exception of Norman McKinnel as John Perry, were felt to be unsatisfactory. Masefield was understandably upset, and refused to allow it to be played again, although it was printed in a limited edition. Vedrenne was equally distressed at the financial, as well as the artistic, failure, and refused ever again to consider a Masefield play. Shaw, on the other hand, despite recognising that it was 'an imperfect dramatic piece', found it very powerful and appalling in its horror. It was he who finally persuaded Vedrenne to think again, and, in fact, the business manager did eventually become involved in the presentation of Masefield's next piece, *The Tragedy of Nan*.

The Tragedy of Nan

Masefield based his next play on a supposedly true story that took place in Kent at the beginning of the nineteenth century. He moved the action to Gloucestershire, a county where the people and places were more familiar to him. Nan Hardwick is an orphan whose father has been hanged for stealing a sheep. She is sent to live with her uncle's family, where she finds scant kindness from her aunt. Mrs Pargetter's dislike of Nan is motivated first, by the fear of social disgrace that the discovery of her father's crime would bring, secondly, by the fact that she was strongly attracted to Nan's father, but was rejected by him, and thirdly, because Nan has won the love of Dick Gurvil, a local boy, who at one time had had a flirtation with Nan's cousin, Jenny. But Mrs Pargetter's concentrated hatred and victimisation of Nan is like John Perry's pathological loathing of his brother in *The Campden Wonder*. The violence of the emotion greatly exceeds the rational grounds on which it is based. Jenny Pargetter feels nothing for Dick Gurvil, but her scheming mother plays on Jenny's shallow self-esteem so that the girl joins her in a plot to tell Dick of Nan's father's disgrace, and thus they prevent the proposed marriage. Nan, who has borne the barrage of insults and deliberate acts of cruelty, like the throwing of her best jacket, a present from her dead father, in the pigswill, breaks under this last blow. She has lost the only person who cared for her. It is then revealed that there has been a miscarriage of justice. Her father was innocent of the crime for which he suffered the death penalty, and she is awarded compensation of £50, making her quite an heiress in the local community. Dick tries to return to his real love, but Nan, recognising his fundamental worthlessness and disregard for women, kills him, in a blow for womankind. She drowns herself, as Mrs Pargetter conceals her inheritance in a kitchen cupboard.

Mrs Pargetter is a monster. Her cruel treatment of Nan, despite the fact that the girl makes every attempt to be of use in her new home, her attempts to alienate Nan from her uncle's affections by accusing her of breaking his favourite mug, her hypocrisy before the parson and her neighbours, and her serving her guests with polluted mutton pies, all bear witness to her utter selfishness and viciousness. Yet she is not only the wicked stepmother of the fairytales, but is at times a terrifying force of evil.

The presentation of human emotion pushed to its limit is not confined to Mrs Pargetter. Nan, herself, is very different from the passive orphan of nineteenth-century melodrama. Although she is represented initially as being quiet and well-behaved, although, despite her own unhappy situation, she is anxious to help those less fortunate, she is not slow to show her defiance against Mrs Pargetter's cruelty, and the running of the coat is followed by a threat to kill the culprit. 'I'll kill you if you tear it.' Her love for Dick Gurvil, although misplaced, is intense and beautifully expressed, 'I feel like my 'eart was in flower, Jenny', she says to her false cousin. And in the same exchange her views on marriage are set in sharp contrast to those of Jenny.

NAN: Did you ever think about men, Jenny? About loving a man? About marriage?

JENNY: I've 'oped to 'ave a 'ome of my own. And not be a
burden 'ere and that.

NAN: Ah! But about 'elping a man?

JENNY: A man 'as strength. 'E ought to 'elp a woman.

NAN: I could 'elp a man, Jenny.

JENNY: Wot ideyers you do 'ave.

Nan implicitly rejects the passive feminine role that Jenny
is pleased to adopt. It is Jenny's betrayal of the good faith in
which Nan confided in her that leads to Nan's revenge –
forcing her cousin to eat the rotten pie that Jenny was
offering to Gaffer Pearce. Nan is no wilting flower of
Victorian womanhood, and when her lover betrays her, her
revenge is fierce, and is elevated into a vindication of all
women who have suffered or who will suffer from mascu-
line egotism.

> You kill people's 'earts. You stamp them in the dust,
> like worms as you tread on the fields. And under it all
> will be the women crying, the broken women, the
> women cast aside. Trampled on. Spat on. As you spat on
> me. No, no, oh, no. Oh young man in your beauty –
> Young man in your strong hunger. I will spare those
> women.

Nan's murder of her faithless lover thus becomes a ritual
slaughter of all vain sensual men who value women
primarily as sexual objects. The raising of Nan's revenge
from the personal to the universal has led critics to claim for
her tragic status, and compare her to Thomas Hardy's
heroine in *Tess of the d'Urbervilles*. Her accusations against
Dick are reminiscent of the ultimate crime man commits
against women in Ibsen's dramas – 'the killing of the love in
her'.

There has been evidence earlier in the play that had the marriage between Nan and Dick taken place, it would not in Hankin's terms have produced 'a happy ending'. There is, for example, a significant gap in the couple's appreciation of the Shavian 'Life Force' that informed or inspired much of the 'new drama':

DICK: I wonder women ever want to 'ave children. They be so beautiful avore they 'ave children. They 'ave their red cheeks, so soft. And sweet lips so red's red. And their eyes bright, like stars a-shining. And oh, such white soft 'ands. Touch one of 'em, and you 'ave like shoots all down. Beau–ti–vul. Love–lee.

NAN: It be a proud thing to 'ave a beauty to raise love in a man.

DICK: And after. I seen the same girls, with their 'ands all rough of washing-day, and their fingers all scarred of stitching. And their cheeks all flaggin', and sunk. And dull as toads' bellies, the colour of 'em. And their eyes be 'eavy, like a foundered wold ewe's when 'er time be on 'er. And lips all bit. And there they do go with the backache on 'em. Pitiful, I call it. Draggin' their wold raggy skirts. And the baby crying. And little Dick with 'is nose all bloody, fallen in the grate. And little Sairey fell in the yard, and 'ad 'er 'air mucked. Ah! Ugh! It go to my 'eart.

NAN: Ah, but that ben't the all of love, Mr Dick. It be 'ard to see beauty gone, and joy gone, and a light 'eart broke. But it be wonderful for to 'ave little ones. To 'ave brought life into the world. To 'ave 'ad them little live things knocking on your 'eart, all of them months. And then to feed them. 'Elpless like that.

DICK: They be pretty, little ones be, when they be kept clean and that. I likes 'earing them sing 'imns. I likes watching the little boys zwimming in the river. They be so white and swift, washing themselves. And the splashin' do shine zo. Diamonds.

Dick's notion of feminine beauty is ideal and conventional, just as the appeal he sees in children lies in their physical attractiveness. He is described early in the play by Mr Pargetter as a philanderer, ('Dick's everybody's man') who needed 'a wife with sense'. Dick's defection from his true love is perhaps rather too sudden to be credible. It might well be the case that he would have broken off with Nan on hearing of her supposedly criminal background that would clearly prejudice his father against him, but it is unlikely that he would so quickly agree to a match with Jenny, in whom in the past he has expressed no more than a passing interest. However, in this piece less than in *The Campden Wonder,* the unlikely incidents in the narrative do not mitigate against the emotional impact of the piece.

Masefield's lyricism is most evident in the speeches of Gaffer Pearce, who has become unbalanced by the premature death of his sweetheart. At his first appearance, his poeticism and his identification of Nan with his doomed love, give him a certain dramatic and poetic power, but the long exchange between them in Act III, when Nan begins to adopt his figurative language becomes self indulgent in its somewhat hackneyed symbolism. William Archer felt on each occasion on which he saw the play, that the third act was unsuccessful, probably because Masefield temporarily loses Nan's character in the somewhat soft-centred maunderings of Pearce. Her own short sentences contain images of simple beauty, and express more feelingly her quiet wisdom. 'There be three times, Dick, when no woman can speak. Beautiful times. When 'er 'ears 'er lover, and when 'er gives 'erself, and when 'er little one is born.'

The play is most successful when the strong passions of the characters are expressed simply and accompanied by the execution of pieces of naturalistic business that are indicated in the stage directions. The opening dialogue between Mrs Pargetter and Jenny takes place while they are rolling dough and cutting apples, Nan resumes the task in tears, after her confrontation with her aunt. In the meantime her uncle consumes the bread and cheese that has been prepared for him. The false 'confidences' scene between Nan and Jenny takes place while they are preparing for the evening party, and the love scene between Nan and Dick is prefaced by the fetching and drinking of cider. The passionate characters are thus placed in a naturalistic setting by the concrete details of ordinary life that surround them, and the mundane properties are used by the characters to express their deep and powerful feelings. The pastry knife that kills Dick has been used for its more usual purpose throughout the play.

The Tragedy of Nan, rejected for the Savoy by Vedrenne, was mounted at the Royalty Theatre on 22 May 1908, by the Pioneer Players, a group of actors including many members of the Court company. Granville Barker directed, and Lillah McCarthy played Nan. Barker was hesitant about his competence to direct a piece, the social *milieu* of which was alien to his own experience, but Lillah McCarthy was very much in tune with setting, which she claimed took her back to her childhood, and she identified strongly with the heroine. It is clear that Lillah McCarthy's passionate style, that was according to Shaw her supreme quality in playing his heroines, was ideally suited to the character. Nan was regarded as one of the finest performances of her career. Shaw was very pleased with the production and was able to persuade Vedrenne to include the play in a series of matinées that he and Barker arranged in association with Harrison at the Haymarket. It was subsequently included in Barker's repertory season at the St James's in 1912.

The play itself is a product of several dramatic traditions. It owes much to Elizabethan Pastoral Tragedy, such as *The Yorkshire Tragedy* and *King John,* and yet it uses some of the features of the 'new drama', like the exploration of women's role in society, the detailed naturalistic settings, the criticism of social institutions such as the Law, that is shown to be in the first place wrong, and in the second, insensitive, and the Church which in the shape of the Parson is exposed as gullible and ultimately self-seeking. The marriage of styles makes an interesting play, not necessarily high tragedy, but certainly powerful drama.

Conclusion

The contribution of the 'new drama' movement to the British theatre was not confined to the provision of plays of high literary and intellectual quality. Most of the writers were closely involved in the presentation of their work on stage and engaged in discussions of current theatrical issues, such as Censorship, the establishment of a National Theatre and the founding of the repertory movement. The impact of the 'new drama' was felt in all aspects of theatre arts, in acting and production, and in the organisation and administration of companies. In setting out to challenge accepted conventional attitudes towards social issues, such as, the role of women, family relationships, the penal system, the ethics of capitalism and the nature of party politics, the 'new dramatists' at the same time made new demands on the theatrical conventions of the nineteenth century. The actor-manager began to evolve into the director; in some companies at least, the dominance of the 'star personality' was replaced by integrated ensemble playing, and the long-run system by some form of repertory. Commercialism and visual splendour were still dominant on the West End stage, but there was now an alternative theatre where the stress was laid on excellent acting and well-written texts.

What began with a small group of intellectual playgoers

watching the production of the banned *Ghosts* in the dingy little Royalty Theatre in 1891 had, by the outbreak of the First World War, developed into the movement that was to set the pattern of theatrical activity in Britain for the rest of the century.

Notes

PART I

The Court Theatre

1. Dinner in Honour of J.E. Vedrenne and Granville Barker, Criterion Restaurant, 7 July 1907. A printed record of the speeches is in the British Library (010325/ff/503).
2. H. Granville Barker and William Archer, *Scheme and Estimates for a National Theatre*, 1907, p. xxiii.
3. Desmond MacCarthy, *The Court Theatre* (1907) p. 15.
4. Lillah McCarthy, *Myself and My Friends* (1933) p.116.
5. Letter from J.L. Shine to G.B. Shaw, 30 October 1904, in *Bernard Shaw: Collected Letters, 1898–1910* Ed. Dan H. Laurence (1972).
6. Margaret Webster, *The Same only Different*, 1969, p. 239
7. Geoffrey Whitworth, *Harley Granville–Barker 1877–1946* (1948) p. 59.
8. Elmer W. Salenius, *Harley Granville Barker* (1983) p. 16.
9. Theodore Stier, *With Pavlova round the World* (1927) p. 257.
10. Sydney Fairbrother, *Through an old Stage–door* (1939) p. 233.
11. Lewis Casson, 'GBS and the Court Theatre', *The Listener*, 12 July 1951.
12. Louis Calvert, *Problems of the Actor* (1919) p. 58.
13. Jean Smith and Arthur Toynbee (eds), *Gilbert Murray, an unfinished autobiography* (1960) p. 153.
14. Lewis Casson, 'GBS at Rehearsal', *Theatrical companion to Shaw*, edited R. Mander and J. Mitchenson (1954) p. 17.

15. Stanley Weintraub, *Shaw – an autobiography, 1898–1950* (1971) p. 32.

16. For a fuller description of the evolution of a naturalistic acting style in the British Theatre, see my article 'New Actors for the New Drama', *Themes in Drama*, VI, 1984.

17. *The Court Theatre*, p. 99.

18. Unidentified review of *John Bull's Other Island*. Enthoven Collection, Victoria and Albert Museum.

19. *Myself and My Friends*, p. 90.

20. Lewis Casson, 'GBS and the Court Theatre', *The Listener*, 12 July 1951.

The Savoy

1. *Shaw/Barker Letters,* ed. C.B. Purdom (1956) p. 104.

Frohman's Repertory Theatre

1. Purdom, p. 98.

2. P.P. Howe, *The Repertory Theatre: a record and a criticism* (1910) p. 154–5.

3. Isaac E. Marcosson and Daniel Frohman, *Charles Frohman* (1916) p. 249.

4. J.P. Wearing, *Letters of Arthur Wing Pinero.* (1974) p. 218.

5. Howe, p. 142.

6. William Archer, 'The Theatrical Situation', *The Fortnightly Review,* n.s. LXXXVIII (1910).

PART II

1.   Granville Barker

1. Geoffrey Whitworth, *What the Theatre owes to Granville Barker,* a reprint of a broadcast (1948) p. 7.

2. G.B. Shaw, 'Granville Barker', *Modern Drama* (1946).

2.   John Galsworthy

1. Letter to Kenneth Andrews, 10 December 1922. Quoted in H.V. Marrot, *The Life and Letters of John Galsworthy* (1935) pp. 790–1.

Notes

2. John Galsworthy, *Glimpses and Reflections,* (1937) p. 93.

3. Marrot, pp. 790–1.

4. Letter to an unrecorded correspondent (10 October 1912). Quoted in Marrot, p. 330.

5. Letter to Granville Barker (19 April 1906). Quoted in Marrot, p. 191.

6. Letter to J.J. Palmer (28 July 1915). Quoted in Marrot, p. 734.

7. Letter to Edward Garnett (10 March 1906). Quoted in Marrot, p. 190.

8. Letter to Granville Barker (19 April 1906). Quoted in Marrot, p. 191.

9. Quoted in Marrot, p. 200.

10. Letter to Edward Garnett (September 1906). Quoted in Marrot, p. 196.

11. Letter to Granville Barker (1 March 1926). Quoted in Marrot, p. 571.

12. Letter to Edward Garnett (10 February 1907). Quoted in Marrot, p. 208.

13. Letter from Garnett to Galsworthy (6 May 1907). Quoted in Edward Garnett, *Letters from John Galsworthy, 1900–1932 (1934) p. 141.*

14. Letter to Gilbert Murray. Quoted in Marrot, p. 213.

15. R.H. Mottram, For Some We Loved (1956) p. 68.

16. Quoted in Marrot, p. 267.

17. Quoted in Marrot, p. 266.

18. Quoted in Marrot, p. 265.

19. Marrot, p. 252–3.

20. Marrot, p. 260.

21. Howe, p. 90.

4. John Masefield

1. Theodore Stier, *With Pavlova round the World* (1927) p. 259.

Bibliography

General Background

Archer, William, *The Old Drama and the New* (Boston: Small, Maynard and Company, 1923).

Howe, P.P., *Dramatic Portraits* (Port Washington, N.Y.: Kennikat Press, 1969).

Jackson, Holbrook, *The Eighteen Nineties* (London: the Harvester Press, 1976).

Morgan, A.E., *Tendencies of Modern English Drama* (New York: Charles Scribner's Sons, 1924).

Nicoll, Allardyce, 'The Play of Ideas: Harley Granville Barker, St John Hankin and John Galsworthy', *English Drama 1900–1930* (Cambridge: Cambridge University Press, 1973).

Trewin, J.C., *The Edwardian Theatre* (Oxford: Blackwell, 1976).

Wilson, A.E., *The Edwardian Theatre* (London: Arthur Baker, 1951).

The Theatres

Goldie, Grace W., *The Liverpool Repertory Theatre 1911–1935* (Liverpool and London, 1935).

Howe, P.P., *The Repertory Theatre: a record and a criticism* (London: Martin Secker, 1910).

Isaac, Winifred F.C., *Alfred Wareing: A Biography* (London, 1948).

Jackson, Anthony, 'Harley Granville Barker as Director the Royal Court Theatre, 1904–1907'. *Theatre Research* 12 (1972).

MacCarthy, Desmond, *The Court Theatre, 1904–1907* (London: 1907).

Miller, Anna Irene, *The Independent Theatre in Europe* (New York, 1931).

Orme, Michael, *J.T. Grein* (London: John Murray, 1936).

Pogson, Rex, *Miss Horniman and the Gaiety Theatre, Manchester* (London, 1952).

Rowell, George and Jackson, Anthony, *The Repertory Movement, a History of Regional Theatre in Britain* (Cambridge: Cambridge University Press, 1984).

Schoenderwoerd, N., *J.T. Grein, Ambassador of the Theatre 1862–1935* (Assen, 1963).

Stokes, John, *Resistible Theatres* (London: Paul Elek Books Ltd, 1972).

The Playwrights and Plays

Barker, Harley Granville, *Three Plays: The Marrying of Ann Leete; The Voysey Inheritance; Waste* (London: Sidgwick and Jackson, 1909).

The Madras House (London: Eyre Methuen, 1977).

The Voysey Inheritance, in *Late Victorian Plays,* ed. George Rowell (London, Oxford and New York, Oxford Paperbacks, 1972).

and Archer, William *Scheme and Estimates for a National Theatre* (London: Duckworth and Co., 1907).

The Exemplary Theatre (London: Chatto and Windus, 1922).

Prefaces to Shakespeare, 2 vols (Princeton: Princeton University Press, 1946–7), 5 vols, (London: Batsford, 1969–71).

Bridge–Adams, W., *The Lost Leader* (London: Sidgwick and Jackson, 1945).

Purdom, C.B. (ed), *Bernard Shaw's Letters to Granville Barker* (London: Phoenix House Ltd, 1956).

Harley Granville Barker: man of the theatre, dramatist and scholar (London: Rockliff, 1955).

Morgan, Margery M., *A Drama of Political Man: a study in the plays of Harley Granville Barker* (London: Sidgwick and Jackson, 1961).

Salenius, Elmer W., *Harley Granville Barker* (Boston: Twayne Publishers, 1982).

Galsworthy, John, *Plays* (London: Duckworth, 1929).

Five Plays, Strife, Justice, The Eldest Son, The Skin Game, Loyalties (London: Methuen, 1984).

Glimpses and Reflections (London: Heinemann, 1937).

The Inn of Tranquillity (London: Heinemann, 1912).

Barker, Dudley, *The Man of Principle: a view of John Galsworthy,* (London: Heinemann, 1963).

Dupont, V., *John Galsworthy: The dramatic artist* (Toulouse and Paris: Didier, n.d.).

Fréchet, Alec, *John Galsworthy: a reassessment* (London: The Macmillan Press, 1982).

Garnett, Edward, *Letters from John Galsworthy, 1900–1932* (London, 1934).

Marrot, H.V., *The Life and Letters of John Galsworthy* (London, 1935).

Hankin, St John, *The Dramatic Works,* Vols 1–3 with introduction by John Drinkwater (London: Martin Secker, 1912).

'Dramatic Sequels', printed in *Punch* from June 1898 – December 1903 (London: Martin Secker, 1926).

Phillips, William H., *St John Hankin: Edwardian Mephistopheles* (London: Associated University Press, 1979).

Masefield, John, *Poems and Plays,* 2 vols (New York: Macmillan Cp., 1918).

The Tragedy of Nan and other plays (London: Heinemann, 1926).

Hamilton, W.H., *John Masefield, A critical study* (London: Macmillan Co., 1922).

Spark, Muriel, *John Masefield* (London and New York: Peter Nevill, 1953).

Index

199